FRONTIERS

FRONTIERS

NEW REVISED EDITION

Ralph Gower

A LION BOOK
Tring · Batavia · Sydney

Published by
Lion Publishing plc
Icknield Way, Tring, Herts, England
ISBN 0 7459 1235 4
Albatross Books Pty Ltd
PO Box 320, Sutherland, NSW 2232, Australia
ISBN 0 86760 861 7

First edition 1983
Reprinted 1984 (twice), 1985
This revised edition 1986
Reprinted 1987

Author's note
The author wishes to make clear that the views expressed in this book are his own, and not necessarily those of the Greater London Council or the Inner London Education Authority

Acknowledgments
The photographs in this book are reproduced by permission of the following photographers and organizations:
Barnaby's Picture Library: pages 8, 12, 13 (above), 17, 19, 26, 29, 31 (both), 34, 37, 38, 41, 47, 54, 55; Fritz Fankhauser: page 52; Sonia Halliday Photographs/Jane Taylor: page 21 (right); Alan Hutchinson Library: pages 67, 72, 81, 93; Lion Publishing/Jon Willcocks: page 13 (below), 50, 61, 84; David Morgan: pages 60, 88; Popperfoto: pages 40, 78; Rex-SIPA Press: pages 32, 34; David Simson: pages 9, 11, 21 (left), 25, 49, 64; Xenon: pages 15 (Libuse Taylor), 46 (Mike Elliott Taylor); Robert Harding: pages 4, 5

Graphics by Tony Cantale

Bible quotations as follows: Ecclesiastes 4:9–10 and Matthew 19:8–9 from *Holy Bible, New International Version*, copyright 1978 New York International Bible Society; all remaining quotations from *Good News Bible*, copyright 1966, 1971 and 1976 American Bible Society, published by Bible Societies/Collins

Other copyright material as follows: Extract from *Cider with Rosie* © 1959 Laurie Lee, first published by The Hogarth Press 1959, published in Penguin Books 1962; extract from *Roots* © 1978 Alex Haley, Hutchinson Publishing Group Ltd

Printed and bound in Spain
D. L. TO:1216 -1987

Contents

Introduction

Some time ago, over 600 children in secondary
schools throughout the Metropolitan Borough of
Sefton, Merseyside, wrote about the kind of
religious education which they believed was relevant
to them and would always be of importance and
interest. Their writing was frank and consistent.
They wanted to know that religion, and the
Christian faith in particular, had something realistic
to say about the issues which they faced. Some of
these were philosophical and theological, such as
'How can people believe in a loving God who allows
evil things to happen?' Most were concerned with
personal and social issues.

This book was written in response to the whole
range of questions which they raised. Although
published some while after their comments were
made, it is hoped that it will meet their needs, and
the needs of others like them, who wish to be sure
about the relevance of their faith.

Ralph Gower

LIFE'S POINTLESS. I'M GOING TO END IT ALL

GO ON— ANOTHER DRINK WON'T HURT

We love each other. What's wrong with sleeping together?

UNIT 1

FRIENDSHIP

One of the legends about Robin Hood tells how he was attracted to an archery contest at Nottingham, drawn by the prize of a silver arrow. Some of his friends in Sherwood Forest— Little John, Will Scarlett and Alan-a-Dale—believed he was walking into a trap, and followed him to the city.

They were right. The Sheriff of Nottingham had planned the contest in the hope that Robin would attend, and had made the contest so difficult that only he could possibly win. Everything went according to plan—Robin Hood was recognized and carried off to the castle to await execution as an outlaw.

Next day, Little John and Will Scarlett attempted to get him out. Dressed as ordinary countrymen, they approached the castle with a deer slung over a pole carried between their shoulders.

'Venison for the kitchens,' shouted Little John to the soldiers who were operating the drawbridge.

Once inside, instead of stopping at the kitchens, they went on to the dungeons. The 'deer' was a skin, stuffed with hay, weapons and tools to release Robin Hood. The guard was overpowered, the cell opened and the shackles broken. Robin Hood got into the skin with the hay and was quickly sewn inside. The three then left for the entrance at the drawbridge.

'Where are you taking the deer?' demanded the guard.

'It wasn't good enough for the Sheriff of Nottingham,' came the reply—and Robin Hood was carried safely out to the freedom of Sherwood Forest.

What is friendship all about?

The legends of Robin Hood are not only good stories—they illustrate friendship, one of the most valuable things in life. But what *is* friendship?

In that escape story, Robin Hood was followed to Nottingham Castle because his friends believed they would be needed. Because they actually *were* needed, they planned and carried out the escape.

The friends who were members of Robin Hood's outlaw group in

❝ A friend in need is a friend indeed. ❞

Sherwood Forest were all fugitives from King John, who ruled England at the time. It was an England where the rich and powerful oppressed the poor. Robin Hood's outlaws wanted to get away from the oppression, but also took money from the wealthy to give to the poor. Their friendship was due to their situation: they were united by a common purpose.

FRIENDSHIP PATTERNS

Imagine there are ten students who are timetabled together. By asking each one of them which person in the group they would most like as their friend, and who would be their second choice, their answers can be recorded as follows:

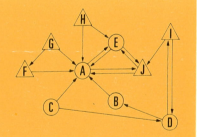

Name	First choice	Second choice
Andrea	Emma	John
Barbara	Christine	Andrea
Christine	Andrea	Dawn
Dawn	Ian	Barbara
Emma	Andrea	John
Fred	Andrea	Christine
Gary	Fred	Andrea
Howard	Andrea	Emma
Ian	John	Dawn
John	Emma	Andrea

If an initial in a circle stands for each girl, and an initial in a triangle for each boy, two arrows can be drawn from the person making the choice to the two they would like to be friends with. Friendship patterns such as these can be represented by a diagram known as a sociogram:

This visual presentation quickly shows up some important facts about the friendship patterns among this group of ten students:

? There is an 'in-group' of three: who are they?

? Who is the most popular of all?

? Who are the isolated ones who nobody wants as friends?

The sociogram gives rise to other questions you may like to discuss, such as:

? What needs are being fulfilled in a group like this?

? How important do you think it is for someone to feel accepted by others?

? What problems can lack of friendship lead to?

As we understand this, we can begin to see what is meant by 'friendship'. We expect friends to be around when we need them—that's what friends are for! It is because friends need one another that we sometimes say we have been 'let down' because our needs have not been met by our friends. Friendship is also experienced by people who share the same interests or aims.

Friendship is a special relationship (outside the family) in which we meet the needs of another person in some way. These 'needs' may be as simple as the need to talk or laugh with someone. When needs are met in this way, we find that we *are* friends, without having to make a special effort to *become* friends.

A shared interest is both a basis for friendship and a way of expressing it.

Making friends

There are three essential elements in friendship, even when it just seems to 'happen':
● having something in common
—same home area or background
—same leisure interests
—same religious beliefs
● telling the other person about ourselves
● finding out about them.

The more that we have in common with somebody, the more likely it is that we will become good friends. Finding out whether we have shared interests and experiences, as a basis for friendship, demands an effort. Someone who is shy, or who worries about the impression he is making, obviously finds it more difficult to make friends than someone who is confident and outgoing.

WHAT THE BIBLE SAYS ABOUT FRIENDSHIP

'Two are better than one, because they have a good return for their work: If one falls down, his friend can help him up.' (Ecclesiastes 4:9–10)

[Jesus said] 'The greatest love a person can have for his friends is to give his life for them.' (John 15:13)

'Friends always show their love. What are brothers for if not to share trouble?' (Proverbs 17:17)

'Some friendships do not last, but some friends are more loyal than brothers.' (Proverbs 18:24)

'A friend means well, even when he hurts you . . .' (Proverbs 27:6)

? What are the characteristics of friendship in each case?
? How might these be expressed practically?

★   ★   ★

'You are my friends if you [trust me enough to] do what I command you.' (John 15:14)

'I do not call you servants any longer, because a servant does not know what his master is doing. Instead, I call you friends, because I have told you everything I have heard from my Father.' (John 15:15)

? Jesus was speaking to his close friends—his 'disciples' or followers—when he said this. What characteristics of friendship did they show to one another?

★   ★   ★

'Even my best friend, the one I trusted most, the one who shared my food, has turned against me.' (Psalm 41:9)

'If it were an enemy that mocked me, I could endure it; if it were an opponent boasting over me, I could hide myself from him. But it is you, my companion, my colleague and close friend.' (Psalm 55:12–13)

? Why do friendships sometimes break up? Why is this a particularly painful experience? How can the damage of a broken friendship be 'repaired'?

LOVE, MARRIAGE AND SEX

Friendship and faith

We have been thinking so far about friendship as a relationship which is outside the family group. This does not mean that people in a family are not friends, but that within a family there is something *more* than friendship. This is sometimes called 'kinship'. We have also seen that people who share a common purpose or the same interests are drawn together and become friends.

These two factors help to explain the strong ties of friendship between people who share the same faith. They have the same deeply-held beliefs, are committed to the same

> Our love should not be just words and talk; it must be true love, which shows itself in action.
> *1 John 3:18*

aims and support and care for one another as a practical way of expressing their friendship.

Christians believe that since Jesus Christ rose from death, he is alive and lives by his Spirit within every Christian today. They therefore share even more than a common belief: they share a common life which makes them into the 'family' of God. So the relationship between Christians is more like kinship—the relationship which exists between members of a family. The New Testament says that Christians are

Making friends with a group of people is difficult. As an outsider wanting to be accepted, do I have to adopt the habits and interests of the group?

members of God's family, having been 'adopted' into it. That is why they can call God 'Father', and why they often call one another 'brother' or 'sister'.

This does not mean that Christians are unfriendly to people who do not share their beliefs! Their new-found relationship with God is expected to lead to helpful and meaningful relationships with other people. They want to share God's love with others. So Christian friendship is most often expressed by meeting other people's needs.
? How have famous Christians—for example, Lord Shaftesbury, Thomas Barnardo, Gladys Aylward and Mother Teresa—shown friendship to people in need?
? How do Christians in your community go about meeting people's needs?

If you had to rearrange the following sets of words into the 'correct' sequence, how would you place them?

● crash   drink   drive
● bury   worry   hurry
● chick   hen   egg
● love   sex   marriage

Some of them are easier to put into order than others. It is often true that someone who drinks and then drives has an accident. Similarly, someone who is always rushing and who worries about things may come to an early death.

The other lists may prove more difficult. How do you decide 'which came first, the chicken or the egg?' And—rather more importantly—which comes first and last in 'love, sex, marriage'?

In some cultures, such as India, where marriages are arranged by parents, the order would be 'marriage, sex, love'. About fifty years ago in the UK, it would have been generally agreed that love should come first, followed by marriage and then sex. Today, marriage often comes the last of the three.
? Which order did you choose, and why?

Love is . . .?

One of the problems with the word 'love' is that we use it to mean so many different things: we love to go to a disco, we love to be with friends, we love cornflakes for breakfast, we love God and we love members of our family.

When we are talking of the love which leads to a married couple setting up home together, we do not mean love in the sense of liking *things*. It is something more than enjoyment or preference. It is also quite different from friendship: we make friends because we have things in common and because we meet each other's needs. Friendship must be present in a marriage, but *in addition to* love.

Another form of love which is very important in marriage is affection. This is fondness or tenderness which gradually grows from being together for a long time. A man might feel affection for a familiar book or his favourite pipe; affection can be felt for the old lady who lives next door. We grow to expect affection from those who are close to us. A marriage without friendship or affection is an empty thing.

But these kinds of love are still quite different from the love we refer to when we say that we have 'fallen in love'. This is not a love which can be easily described or explained because it is not rational. It is a desire and a longing to be completely united with another person. It is a complete preoccupation with him or her, as distinct from any pleasure or happiness which they can give to us. Even if they turn us down, or cause us unhappiness, we continue to love them.

Falling in love demands a certain level of emotional maturity, normally reached in teen-age. It should not be confused with 'infatuation', which is an immature and overpowering feeling for someone which can lead to extravagant and ill-judged actions. True love puts the other person first, and treats them with care and respect.

The New Testament of the Bible, which was written in Greek, used a number of words for 'love', so that the different forms of it could be easily distinguished:
● *philos*—friendship
● *storgê*—affection
● *eros*—falling in love/sexual attraction
● *agape*—self-sacrificing, sharing love.

Sexual relationships
Arousing the sex instinct can lead to powerful emotions: pleasure, frustration, love, hate, desire, revulsion. So sex means more than physical feelings: it involves deep emotions; it changes people.

There are a number of levels at which contact can be made:
1 Sight, hearing or smell.
2 Simple touch—holding hands, putting arm round waist or shoulders.
3 Kissing.
4 Intimate touch—bare body, especially breasts and sex organs.
5 Union of sex organs.

There are several important characteristics of the levels of sexual contact:
● They are **progressive**. You first become conscious of someone's 'sex appeal' through the shape of their body, the sound of their voice or perhaps the smell of their perfume! The sex appeal may eventually lead to sexual union, but normally only

---

❛ A girl plays at sex for which she is not ready, because fundamentally what she wants is love; and the boy plays at love, for which he is not ready, because what he wants is sex. ❜
Mary Calderone

---

over a period of time, through stages which correspond to the levels listed.
● They represent **levels of arousal**. It is easy to draw back from a person when the level of contact is low, but it is very difficult to draw back at higher levels of contact—for example, once level 4 has been reached—because of the degree of sexual arousal.
● When people are attracted to one another, there is a **level of commitment**. It begins with interest and friendship, and might proceed to 'going steady', falling in love and marriage. Most people would say that there should be a

correspondence between the level of commitment and the level of sexual contact.

Points of view
People hold many different points of view about sex inside and outside marriage today:
● When two people are in love, sexual union is the closest way they have of being 'one' with each other. It's the ultimate way of saying 'I love you'. So, sexual intercourse is a mark of close friendship and is OK between people who love each other.
● The sex instinct is an 'appetite' which needs satisfying, like hunger or thirst. So, whenever there is the opportunity to meet this need, casual sex with any partner is OK.
● Sexual union needs the security and commitment of marriage, where every aspect of life is shared together. As well as for conceiving children, it is for celebration, for comfort, for giving, for fun, for expression of the longing to be united—and all this cannot be fulfilled outside marriage.

What are your own points of view?
? What levels of commitment should correspond to the levels of sexual contact? Why?
? What are the dangers of the 'casual sex' viewpoint?

'Till death us do part'?
Marriage is an arrangement made by two people to live together, so that they can express their love in daily life, with social approval and support. 'Living together' is marriage *without* family and community approval and support. In some societies, marriage is regarded as having taken place when a price is

The percentage of weddings held in churches and register offices

	1966	1971	1975	1980
Church weddings	68	60	53	50
Civil weddings	32	40	47	50

? Marriage itself is still a very popular institution. Why do you think this is so?

? Why are fewer church weddings taking place?
? Why do you think that some marriages do not survive?

paid for the bride, or when the marriage is 'consummated', that is, sexual intercourse has taken place.

In the West, a marriage usually takes place when a declaration of a couple's intention to live together for life, to the exclusion of all others, is made to a person in authority—a registrar or his representative, a clergyman or sometimes the captain of a ship. Many people would not want to take such an important step without involving God. In such a case, the marriage begins with a religious ceremony, in which the bride and groom make their promises to one another before God, and his help is asked to enable the couple to keep their vows.

Although it has been traditional to have a 'church wedding', the religious ceremony—in Britain at least—is declining in popularity.

Christian marriage

If a wedding is held in a Christian church, there are normally six parts to the service, although these may differ from one denomination to another:

- a statement of what marriage is for;
- questions asked of witnesses, the bride and groom to make sure that they can be legally married;
- questions asked of the bride and groom to see if they *wish* to be married;
- the marriage itself: the bride's father (or his representative) gives his daughter into the care of the groom, who receives her; the bride then receives the groom, and a ring or rings are exchanged to seal the agreement;

MARRIAGE IN WORLD FAITHS

Judaism

Although the Old Testament contains many stories of men with more than one wife, the general practice was one man, one wife. To endorse this, the rabbis point out that God gave Adam only one wife. It is also interesting to see that the *Talmud*, a record of 1,000 years of Jewish learning, only refers to 'a wife', never 'wives'.

A Jewish wedding today starts when the groom places a ring on the bride's finger and says, 'Be sanctified to me with this ring in accordance with the laws of Moses and Israel.' It is this act which makes her his wife. A contract, which has been drawn up between the bride and groom before the ceremony, is then read to the congregation, declaring how the groom will support his wife. Next, the couple stand beneath a canopy while seven benedictions, or prayers of thanksgiving to God, are recited.

During the ceremony, prayers are said over a cup of wine, and the bride and groom drink from the cup. Finally, a small glass is smashed so that everyone present will remember the destruction of the temple in Jerusalem in AD 70.

Sexual relationships are a very important part of marriage to the Jew. Standing beneath the canopy symbolizes consummation, and following the ceremony, the bride and groom always go to a private room by themselves. The sexual relationship is not only for the bringing of children into the world, but to express unity together, for enjoyment and for love.

Islam

In a Muslim community, sexual relationships are kept strictly within marriage, and there is severe punishment for any transgression of this. For this reason, in many Muslim countries, women in public are sombrely dressed and veiled so that they do not constitute a temptation to men.

Not only is there no sexual relationship outside marriage, but there is no courtship either. Most marriages are arranged by parents. The bride is chosen, ideally, for her religious life and piety, and not for her good looks or wealth. It is possible, when young people first meet, for them to go against the wishes of their parents, but it is not usual.

A Muslim man is allowed to take up

Muslim women have traditionally worn modest dress. The idea is being revived in countries which want to become truly Islamic states.

to four wives. If he does so, the *Qur'an* says that he has to treat them all equally—providing for them equally in every way. Within marriage, sexual intercourse is intended for having children rather than for enjoyment, so family planning methods are not normally used in a Muslim country.

Hinduism

Marriages are arranged for young people in the Hindu community. Relatives and friends look for a suitable match: a partner of similar age, outlook and status. Someone outside the family introduces the young people concerned. It is also possible for young people to make their own introductions and to marry with the agreement of their parents, but this only happens in about one in ten marriages.

At one time a dowry was given to the couple to give them a good start in making their home, but modern practice has changed the custom. The girl's family now give gifts to members of the boy's family.

Marriages are very stable among Hindus, for two reasons. First, Hindus believe that Brahma, God, is everything and is in everything. He is therefore in the husband as well as in the wife. The Hindu will therefore sometimes say, 'I love my wife because she is me'. Why quarrel with yourself? The other reason is that to achieve *karma* (a good balance which will result in a better life in a future existence) it is important to do one's duty, and being a dutiful husband or wife is part of that.

All spiritual matters are looked after by the husband. As within the Muslim community, sex relationships are kept within marriage, and family planning is rarely practised.

'TO HAVE AND TO HOLD . . .'

'I do solemnly declare that I know not of any lawful impediment why I, . . ., may not be joined in matrimony to . . .'
Legal requirement in all services

'I call upon these persons here present to witness that I, . . ., take you, . . ., to be my lawful wedded husband; to have and to hold, from this day forward, for better for worse, for richer for poorer, in sickness and in health, to love, cherish and to obey, while life shall last; according to God's holy law, and to this I pledge myself.'
From a Baptist service book

'. . . and . . . have together made their covenant before God and this company; they have made their vows to each other and have shown their consent by the giving and receiving of rings. Therefore I pronounce them husband and wife in the Name of the Father and of the Son and of the Holy Spirit. Those whom God has joined together, let no man put asunder.'
From a Methodist service book

A church wedding is two ceremonies for the price of one: the legal requirements of the state are met, and promises are made before God.

● a declaration is made that in God's sight they are married;
● prayers are said, asking God to help the couple to be faithful to one another and to help them throughout their married life.

At some time during the service, the bride and the groom sign their names in a register before several witnesses, and a certificate to say that the marriage has been entered in the register is given to the bride.

What the Bible says about marriage

The Christian marriage service is based on a number of beliefs about marriage drawn from the Bible.
● **Two people become one** A man and a woman leave their parents and become 'one flesh' together. This was the original point of marriage as created by God. It was upheld by Jesus, and taught by Paul. The original aim was both for companionship and to have children. (Bible references for further study: Genesis 2:18–24; Matthew 19:3–6)
● **A man should have one wife** Although several wives were allowed in Bible times, the ideal was always one man with one woman, from outside the immediate family. More than one wife could bring problems either for the husband or for the wives. (Bible references: Deuteronomy 21:15–17; 27:20–23; 1 Samuel 1:1–18)
● **Sex relationships should be confined to marriage** A woman was expected to be a virgin before marriage and sex relations outside marriage were forbidden. Even the thought of having sex with someone outside marriage was wrong by Christ's standards. Perversion was also forbidden. (Bible references: Exodus 20:14; Deuteronomy 5:18; 22:12–21; 2 Samuel 11–12; Proverbs 7:6–27; Matthew 5:27–28; Romans 1:26–27)
● **There are different roles for husband and wife** Husband and wife are interdependent: they have different strengths, abilities and characteristics, and should complement each other and provide mutual support. (Bible references: Genesis 2:18–25; Ephesians 5:21–33)
● **Marriage should be permanent** Divorce was allowed by the Old Testament law because of human sinfulness. Jesus allowed it too, but stressed the original ideal for man and woman as created by God. Christians believe that when their lives are dedicated to God, then God brings the right people together. This does not mean that they never experience any problems in their marriages, but they believe that God gives the kind of love which makes it possible for a marriage to survive. (Bible references: Deuteronomy 24:1; Matthew 5:31–32; 19:7–9; Romans 7:1–3; 1 Corinthians 7:10–15; 13:4–7)

Christians, marriage and sex

While most Christians would agree with those four points, some are stricter about their interpretation than others. For example, the Roman Catholic Church does not allow divorce; Roman Catholics also believe that sexual intercourse is for bringing children into the world, not simply for enjoyment, so the use of any artificial means of contraception is forbidden.

All Christians hold to the fundamental teaching of the Bible that full sexual expression should be reserved solely for one's marriage partner. The creation stories in the first book of the Bible, Genesis, teach that intercourse:
● was made by God to strengthen and protect relationships;
● makes two people 'become one person';
● is the seal on two people's exclusive and permanent

commitment to each other for life—i.e. marriage.

It is for these very positive reasons that Christians insist that the right place for intercourse is within marriage. Casual sex means treating someone like a sex-object rather than a complete personality, and in so doing, using them for temporary, selfish satisfaction. Even those who go to bed together to express close friendship are treating intercourse as something *less* than God intended. They are trying to become 'one flesh' without the security or long-term commitment of marriage (for it takes time to get to know how to love one another), and with the danger of tearing the relationship apart again when the affair is over, with the emotional problems that must follow.

Christians are not being 'killjoys' or 'old-fashioned' when they say 'No sex before marriage'. In fact, Christian teaching can come as a real liberation to those who have been trying to find fulfilment in casual sex, or who feel they are missing out because 'everyone's doing it'. The Bible shows the way men and women have been *designed* to behave. So Christians recognize sexual instincts as God-given and want to fulfil them in the best possible context—the stable commitment of marriage.

Assignments and discussion topics

1 Most of the letters on the problem pages of magazines relate to love, marriage and sex. Find some examples of readers' questions and then try to write your own answers. Discuss your 'solutions' to the writers' problems.

2 Try to find examples of both classical and modern poetry, pop-song lyrics, etc, which are on the theme of love. Why do you think love is such a popular theme for poets and song-writers? What kinds of 'love' do they describe?

3 Find examples of modern advertising which appeal to people's sex instincts in trying to sell particular products and discuss them.

UNIT 3

THE FAMILY

These two pictures of families were taken approximately 100 years apart. The style of photography is obviously different; so are the styles of clothing and hair.

There is another big difference, too: there are many more people in the older picture. Of course, families had a larger number of children a century ago, but there was also a different idea of what 'family' meant. Everyone descended from one set of grandparents were all part of one family: grandparents, aunts, uncles and cousins, as well as parents and children.

Today, in the West, when we say 'family', we are usually referring to just the parents and children. The larger family is sometimes called the 'extended' family, and the smaller one the 'nuclear' family.
? What advantages might an extended family arrangement have?
? What could some of its disadvantages be? (For both questions, think in terms of *all* members of the family group.)

What is a family?

What do we mean by a family? Some people have said simply that 'a family is the group that someone grows up in'. But that clearly does not tell us enough. It is true for a child, but not for an adult. It is what the family actually *does* that makes it so important:
● When we are growing up, the family teaches us **what is expected of us in society**, what language we should use, what attitudes we should have, what forms of behaviour are acceptable.
● When we are growing up, the family shows us our **place in society** in relation to other people. This is especially important in Hindu society, for example, where there are four main social groupings,

or 'castes'. A child born into a particular caste keeps that caste for life, and is taught by the family how to behave towards members of other castes.

● When we are very young, the family influences **the kind of person we will become**. If parents bring their child up too strictly and without much affection, he is likely to grow up very insecure and fearful. If a child is given too much freedom, he finds it difficult to fit into society when he grows up. If parents reject their children, the children tend to be anti-social and get into trouble. If one or other of the parents is absent for a long period, their children may find it difficult to relate to other adults later in life.

● The family gives us a **sense of identity**. This is important for both parents and children. It is the group to which a person belongs, which supports him in making decisions and when things go wrong. It is the group which first shares our joys and sorrows. It is the group where we should always find affection and care.

Can the family survive?

Sociologists have suggested several reasons why the family unit might not survive:

● **A family is too expensive** With the high cost of living, a couple may not be able to afford to have children. Or they may not wish to 'pay the price' of restricting their

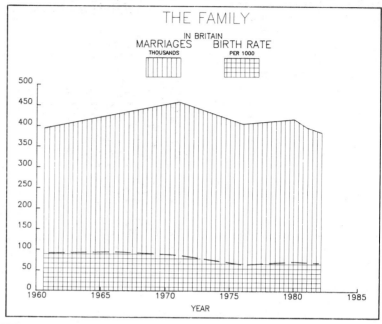

WHAT THE BIBLE SAYS ABOUT THE FAMILY

'Jesus said . . . "In the beginning, at the time of creation, 'God made them male and female,' as the scripture says. 'And for this reason a man will leave his father and mother and unite with his wife, and the two will become one.' So they are no longer two, but one. Man must not separate, then, what God has joined together." (Mark 10:6–9)
Family life was created by God and endorsed by Jesus.

★   ★   ★

' "The Lord—and the Lord alone—is our God. Love the Lord your God with all your heart, with all your soul, and with all your strength. Never forget these commands that I am giving you today. Teach them to your children . . ." ' (Deuteronomy 6:4–7)
Children were taught about God in the family.

★   ★   ★

' "When a man is newly married, he is not to be drafted into military service or any other public duty; he is to be excused from duty for one year, so that he can stay at home and make his wife happy." ' (Deuteronomy 24:5)
Among the Israelites, priority was given to the establishment of marriage and family life.

★   ★   ★

' "If two brothers live on the same property and one of them dies, leaving no son, then his widow is not to be married to someone outside the family; it is the duty of the dead man's brother to marry her. The first son that they have will be considered the son of the dead man, so that his family line will continue in Israel." ' (Deuteronomy 25:5–6)
This 'Levirate law' of the Old Testament protected the family.

★   ★   ★

'When Joseph and Mary had finished doing all that was required by the law of the Lord, they returned to their home town of Nazareth in Galilee. The child grew and became strong; he was full of wisdom, and God's blessings were upon him.' (Luke 2:39–40)
Jesus was born and grew up in a family.

★   ★   ★

'Children, it is your Christian duty to obey your parents, for this is the right thing to do. "Respect your father and mother" is the first commandment that has a promise added: "so that all may go well with you, and you may live a long time in the land." Parents, do not treat your children in such a way as to make them angry. Instead, bring them up with Christian discipline and instruction.' (Ephesians 6:1–4)
There are obligations for both parents and children if family life is to function well.

★   ★   ★

'If anyone does not take care of his relatives, especially the members of his own family, he has denied the faith and is worse than an unbeliever.' (1 Timothy 5:8)
Family members have a responsibility to care for one another.

own freedom by having family commitments. Whatever the reason, family planning techniques have made it possible for people to avoid or delay having a family.

● **The family is no longer needed** Its functions have been taken over by others. The teaching function of the family—even in areas such as health and sex education—has been taken over by the schools.

(Your family are the people who have to take you back when you have to go back to them.)
Teenager

The providing function is also increasingly being fulfilled by the social services, leaving less reason for family members to care for each other's needs.

● **Changing attitudes** Extramarital sex poses a threat to the stability of the traditional family unit. It is also increasingly common for couples to live together without getting married: they are 'married' in 'common law' but without long-term commitment or security, and without the recognition of family or community.

● **The roles of parents are changing** The familiar pattern of father being the bread-winner and mother doing the cooking, cleaning, shopping and bringing up the children, no longer applies in many families. Women are encouraged to enter the world of work too and to expect help from their husbands at home. Some people feel that the resulting changed relationships may bring about the disappearance of the family.

Changes and challenges

The kibbutz is a change in the pattern of family life rather than the end of it. It is not the first time that such a change has taken place.

In prehistoric times, the basic grouping was the 'village family': the men hunted for food and the women searched for grain. The food and grain were brought back to the village. A major change took place when people realized that it would be

AN ALTERNATIVE FAMILY?

A family is not the only way that a group of people can live together. One alternative is a commune, such as the kibbutz in Israel, where a large number of families and singles all choose to live together.

In a kibbutz, each person has one job which is performed for the rest of the community. Some jobs—in agriculture or industry—provide the community with an income: picking bananas, growing maize, cutting plywood or making furniture. Other jobs keep the community going: washing clothes, preparing meals, cleaning apartments, teaching children and caring for babies. Everyone decides together how the community should be organized and how the income from agriculture and industry should be spent.

The most unusual feature of the organization of the kibbutz is that it does away with the family as we know it. Babies are cared for by trained nurses. The parents start work at 6 a.m. each day, return at about 2 p.m., have a meal in the communal dining-room, then return to their apartment (which has been cleaned for them). After they have had a rest, their baby comes home for a short time before going back to the nursery. As the child grows, he will spend more and more time with his parents. When he leaves the nursery, he will sleep in a dormitory with other boys and girls; when he is older still, he will have a room of his own.

People who live on a kibbutz say that the system works well because

Children on a kibbutz live separately from their parents so that they can be looked after during the day while their parents are at work. What do you think are the advantages and disadvantages of this arrangement? Why are some of the kibbutzim now changing to the traditional family pattern of children living with parents?

parents actually spend more time with their children than happens in Western society, where parents are often so busy doing household jobs that they never actually give their undivided attention to their children. Critics of the kibbutz say that the children find it difficult to relate easily to adults.

Whatever its pros and cons, the kibbutz does not signal the end of the family. It is another type of family.

better to grow the grain seeds in a field, and to tame some of the animals for use by the household.

This 'domestication' of plants and animals around 3000 BC has been called the 'Neolithic Revolution' because of its far-reaching impact on the organization of society. This development meant that the small family units had to leave the safety of the village and build their own homes near to their fields and herds. It was a complete change of family life-style, but the family unit—now a 'household family'—was still intact.

The other major change took place at the time of the Industrial Revolution in nineteenth-century Europe. Up to this time, families had

worked together on their piece of land: the men and boys did the heavy work of ploughing, women did the planting or milking, children looked after the smaller animals. Wool from the sheep was spun and woven on the farm, and care and education were provided within the family. Other needs were met through the sale of produce at the local market.

However, when machines took over from craft work, factories were built, and it became necessary for some members of the family to leave home to work at the factory. The family changed completely, but it survived in a different form.

This form of family is with us still, but there are pressures which make it look as if things will change yet again. Can the family respond to the current challenges and adapt to the new demands being made of it?

Assignments and discussion topics

1 Write the names of everyone in a family you know, or invent names for the people in a photograph in this unit. Opposite each name, write what each person does in the family and what you think each person *ought* to do. In a family, do we tend to be more conscious of our *rights* rather than our *responsibilities*?

2 Write down twenty jobs which regularly need doing in a home (shopping, gardening, cleaning the car, mending . . .). Opposite each job, write which member(s) of the family should do them. Be prepared to discuss and defend your answers!

3 American researchers have described the different types of leadership in families as 'father-dominated', 'father-led', 'equality' and 'mother-dominated'. They found that 'father-led' families had the most stable and happy children. Why do you think this should be so? Do you agree?

4 What issues cause the most arguments in your family? How are the arguments resolved?

5 It has been said that the three elements necessary for bringing up a family are love, discipline and freedom. Why are *all three* necessary? How should they be exercised?

6 If and when you have your own family, what will you do the same as/differently from your parents?

7 Why should a Christian faith make a difference to family life?

UNIT 4

DIVORCE

A hundred and fifty years ago, it was almost impossible for a person to obtain a divorce in the UK. Now it is so commonplace that there are well over 100,000 divorces every year. Even though divorce is so common, every statistic represents heartbreak and upset for someone who once believed that their married happiness was going to last for life.

Divorce and the law

Until 1969—when the Divorce Law Reform Act was passed in the British parliament—divorce was granted on the grounds that one of the partners had committed an offence against the marriage. The offences had grown in number over a period of 120 years.

In 1857, a man could obtain a divorce if he could prove that his wife had committed adultery. In 1878, a woman could obtain a separation from her husband if she could prove that his cruelty was an offence against the marriage. Not until 1923 could the husband or wife sue for divorce on equal terms. By 1937, desertion and insanity had been added to the list.

This meant that divorce proceedings were always unpleasant: proof had to be given to a court that the other marriage partner had been unfaithful, cruel, a deserter or was insane. It was sometimes said that if the relationship between husband and wife was strained before the court hearing, it was destroyed after it.

Many people began to feel that a change in the law was needed. They believed that divorce should be granted *not* because a partner to the marriage had done something wrong, but because it could be shown that the marriage had broken down and could not be repaired. This was the major change brought in by the Divorce Law Reform Act of 1969. A

court now has to be satisfied that this 'irretrievable breakdown' has been caused because of adultery, unreasonable action, desertion or separation. At each step, attempts are to be made to bring about reconciliation between husband and wife.

Although some people feel that this change in the law has made divorce easier, others say that it has led to no more marriage breakdowns—marriages were breaking down before the 1969 Act, but they had just not been legally dissolved.

Marriage breakdown in Western society

There are many pressures on marriage in our society:

● **Finance** In an age of high inflation, there may be insufficient money to meet the rent or mortgage, pay for fuel and provide food and clothing. This leads to worry and tension, which people tend to work out on those closest to them.

● **Lack of companionship** Solutions to the financial worries sometimes lead to more problems. If the wife decides to go out to work, or the husband does shift work or overtime to ease the money situation, there are often strains in the relationship. After work, the wife still has jobs to do at home when she is tired; if the husband is away, or asleep when she is at home, there is a loss of time to talk together. Companionship is much more important in marriage than most people realize—a prolonged illness or long periods of separation because of work commitments can also place great strains on a marriage.

● **Lack of communication** Both partners can be so busy that they never spend time just telling each other how they feel, what they think, what they have been doing. Some do not find it easy to express themselves, and this too can lead to misunderstanding.

● **Great expectations** Marriage is being expected to fulfil an increasing number of needs—friendship, romance, exciting sex, comfort, advice, a measure of independence, personal development and so on. People can become disillusioned and

DIVORCE IN THE UK

	1971	1972	1973	1974	1975	1976	1979	1981	1983
Number of thousands of divorces in the UK (1951–31; 1961–27; 1980–158)	80	125	114	121	129	136	148	157	162
Number of thousands of divorces in England & Wales with families of:									
No children under 16	32	52	42	45	47	49	54	60	N/A
1 child under 16	17	27	24	26	28	30	31	33	
3 or more children under 16	10	16	16	16	18	18	14	13	
Number of thousands of marriages per year in:									
Church of England	160	156	144	138	133	120		N/A	N/A
Register Office	180							N/A	N/A
Between divorcees	71			100	104	113		122	N/A
Percentages of total number of divorces within given years of marriage:									
Up to 4 years	13	13	16	16	17	18		19	21
5/9 years	30	28	29	30	30	30		30	29
10/14 years	19	18	19	19	18	19		19	19
15/19 years	13	13	13	13	13	13		12	13
20 or more years	24	27	23	22	21	20		19	18

? Why do you think there was a rapid rise in the number of divorces in the 1970s?
? Is there any evidence to show that parents sometimes stay together for the sake of the children?

? Why do you think that marriages in the Church of England have become less popular, while marriages in the Register Office have become more popular?

? Why do you think that the periods between 5 and 9 years after marriage, and after 20 years of marriage are more likely to lead to divorce than other periods?

disenchanted when their marriage does not come up to scratch.

● **The media** Newspapers, popular novels, cinema and television all use unfaithfulness in marriage as part of their excitement or entertainment. Extra-marital sex is portrayed as the norm, and this view is often accepted by the readers and viewers. A couple having problems with their marriage may well not feel so worried about adopting the same standards themselves, since society has come to accept such patterns of behaviour.

● **Change** When someone gets married at seventeen or eighteen, he/she will have changed significantly by the time they reach, say, twenty-five. So if their marriage partner were to say to them 'You're not the person I married!' in many ways that would be quite right. When children arrive, there may be a change of house, a change of job, new friends.

Broken marriage relationships and divided families cause hardship and suffering. Life is not easy for the single parent with the responsibility of bringing up children alone.

In different situations, people sometimes behave in a different way.

● **No family** Children make a lot of difference to the stability of a marriage. Parents know that the children need their support, so for the children's sake, they stay together when otherwise tensions would lead to complete breakdown. Children often provide a common interest for parents too—another reason for staying together. When the children have left home, and the common interest is not there, the marriage may be in danger of coming to grief.

The aftermath

Novels and films bring out the excitement of an extra-marital affair, but rarely go on to show the heartache for the person who has been let down.

There are many problems which have to be faced when the divorce is over and life has to be started over again:

● **Emotional** Marriage breakdown itself is a great emotional trauma, but the strain does not end in the divorce court. Wondering how old friends will react and 'beginning life again' as a single person is very stressful for the divorcee.

● **Financial** Legal proceedings cost money and the arrangements made in court for maintenance payments can cause severe financial hardship. It is always more expensive to keep two homes instead of one. It can be difficult for the parent who has custody of the children to find a suitable job.

● **Children** Children of a divorced couple are usually 'innocent victims' of a situation they do not really understand. They have to live with one parent (usually their mother) most of the time and see the other parent on visits. This can lead to feelings of insecurity and sometimes to behavioural problems.

● **Social** Divorcees may not find it easy to have a normal social life. It is not much fun going out on your own. In a society geared to couples, he/she may get left out of invitations because of making an odd number. The single parent has the additional problem of finding babysitters.

DIVORCE IN HINDUISM AND ISLAM

The view of marriage held by the society to which we belong is an important factor in whether a marriage is likely to last. If a couple get married with the idea that 'if things don't work out, we can always get a divorce', there is no strong foundation for the marriage. In societies where divorce is not allowed, there are far fewer marriage breakdowns, because when things are not going smoothly, the couple know that they must make things work. There is no alternative. The views of society are very important in Hindu and Muslim communities, for example, but the pressures are of a different kind from those experienced in the West.

The Hindu believes that if he lived a good life in a previous existence upon earth, then not only will he have a higher status in society in this life, but he will get a good marriage partner as well. To admit that his marriage partner is bad is to admit that his previous life was bad too. He therefore believes that his wife is good, and the marriage harmonious.

Apart from this, Hindu marriages are arranged by parents who are very careful to see that the couple will get on together. While this seems strange in Western society, the Hindu would say, 'We do not choose our parents, so why should we choose our wives?'

However, divorce is not impossible. If the husband is very cruel, or if there are no children after fifteen years of marriage, the marriage can be dissolved.

In Islam there is pressure of a different kind, because a man marries not just the woman, but her family as well. This is part of the Muslim emphasis on community. As well as this, the hope for companionship in marriage is not always very high, so there is little risk of disappointment. The *Qur'an* allows divorce after a man has said three times 'I divorce thee' to his wife. It urges a lot of hard thinking before such action is taken. These combined factors lead to a much lower divorce rate than is common in the Western world.

WHAT THE BIBLE SAYS ABOUT DIVORCE

The Law
' "Suppose a man marries a woman and later decides that he doesn't want her, because he finds that she is guilty of some shameful conduct. So he writes out divorce papers, gives them to her, and sends her away from his home." ' (Deuteronomy 24:1)

● *Divorce allowed for 'some shameful conduct'. Some Jewish rabbis took this to mean adultery; others said it could be anything that upset the husband, such as burning his dinner!*

● *Divorce was not made easy. A certificate of divorcement had to be drawn up and given by the husband to his wife (even when he was in the wrong). This is still the practice in the Jewish community.*

● *Remarriage after divorce was allowable.*

★   ★   ★

The teaching of Jesus
' "Man must not separate . . . what God has joined together." ' (Mark 10:9)

[Jesus said] ' "Moses permitted you to divorce your wives because your hearts were hard. But it was not this way from the beginning. I tell you that anyone who divorces his wife, except for marital unfaithfulness, and marries another woman commits adultery." ' (Matthew 19:8–9)

● *God's ideal for marriage does not include divorce.*

● *God allowed Moses to legislate for divorce because of breakdowns in relationships.*

● *Sexual unfaithfulness is allowed as a proper ground for making a new start.*

★   ★   ★

The teaching of Paul
'If a Christian man has a wife who is an unbeliever and she agrees to go on living with him, he must not divorce her. And if a Christian woman is married to a man who is an unbeliever and he agrees to go on living with her, she must not divorce him . . .
However, if the one who is not a believer wishes to leave the Christian partner, let it be so. In such cases the Christian partner, whether husband or wife, is free to act.' (1 Corinthians 7:12–13, 15)

● *God's ideal of marriage for life is restated.*

● *If a Christian is deserted by a partner who does not share his/her faith, the Christian is free to divorce and remarry.*

Key issue

Different branches of the Christian church interpret the Bible passages about divorce in different ways. Some Christians, including the Roman Catholic Church, take the strict view and do not allow divorce or remarriage at all. They believe that the vows taken at the marriage service, and the physical union which follows, can never be broken. They believe that this was the way God planned it, and so he gives special help to enable people to live up to that standard.

An option for divorcees who wish to remarry in church is to have a Register Office wedding followed by a 'service of blessing' in a church. Despite experiencing the pain of a marriage breakdown, three out of every four divorcees in Britain choose to get married again.

Until recently, the Church of England has taken the view that while divorce is allowable, there can be no subsequent remarriage. It is felt that divorce is better than separation—for example, for the battered or abused wife—because it provides some security. However, views have been changing and, at the discretion of individual vicars and with a bishop's permission, divorcees are sometimes able to remarry in church.

Some Christians hold what is called the 'lenient view'—that there can be both divorce and remarriage. They accept that Jesus said that remarriage was sometimes allowable after divorce, and therefore allow remarriage at least to the 'innocent party' and sometimes to others, too. They feel that this is a way of showing God's attitude to us—the

offer of forgiveness and a chance to make a new start.

Despite differences of opinion on divorce and remarriage, all Christians would agree on the importance of marriage, and that all possible attempts at reconciliation should be made when things go wrong. They also seek to show love and understanding to those who have been hurt by the experience of a divorce.

Discussion topics

1 If marriage is such a mine-field, should it be abolished? Or can anything be done to help potential partners detect the 'mines', the possible trouble-spots, beforehand?

2 Do you think that 'easy divorce' means that people do not make an effort to work through the bad patches in their marriage?

3 Should divorce and remarriage be made even easier?

4 Why do you think that so many divorced people opt to get married again?

5 What particular problems do single parent families have to face?

In the ancient Greek world, the philosopher Socrates was condemned to commit suicide by drinking hemlock because he was found guilty of corrupting the youth of Athens by his questions. Queen Cleopatra of Egypt allowed herself to be bitten by a snake when she heard that her husband, Antony, had been defeated in battle. In the Bible, King Saul of Israel committed suicide rather than be tortured by the Philistines, and Judas Iscariot took his own life when he realized that his betrayal was going to result in Jesus' death.

More recently, on Captain Scott's expedition to the South Pole, one of the party, Captain Oates, walked out into a blizzard rather than endanger the lives of all the rest. Marilyn Monroe, one of the twentieth century's most successful film stars, is thought to have taken her own life.

As well as the rich and famous, there are many ordinary people who attempt to take their own lives. In the UK alone, there are about 100,000 people who try to commit suicide every year; about 4,000 of them succeed.

Reasons for suicide

There are many circumstances which can bring people to the point of feeling so desperate that they decide to 'end it all'. What reasons can you think of?

● **Loneliness** It is easy to assume that people who attempt to commit suicide do so because they simply cannot cope with life. But the truth is deeper than this. The bankruptcy, the unwanted pregnancy, the broken romance or the drug dependence is a major problem in itself—but on top of this, there is no one to talk to about it. People have to face their problems alone. A suicide attempt may be a desperate cry for help when

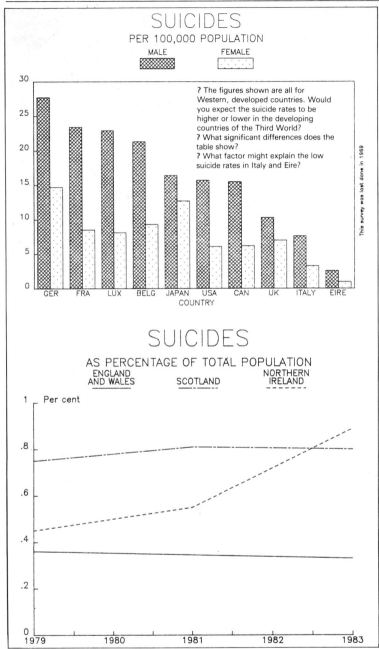

SUICIDES
PER 100,000 POPULATION

MALE   FEMALE

? The figures shown are all for Western, developed countries. Would you expect the suicide rates to be higher or lower in the developing countries of the Third World?
? What significant differences does the table show?
? What factor might explain the low suicide rates in Italy and Eire?

This survey was last done in 1969

GER FRA LUX BELG JAPAN USA CAN UK ITALY EIRE
COUNTRY

SUICIDES
AS PERCENTAGE OF TOTAL POPULATION

ENGLAND AND WALES   SCOTLAND   NORTHERN IRELAND

Per cent

1979   1980   1981   1982   1983

someone feels that nobody cares about them.

● **Mental illness** Most people try to commit suicide because they have the illness called 'depression'. It is important to realize that when people are mentally ill, they cannot be blamed for attempting to commit suicide. Their illness prevents them from knowing what they are doing. Often it is a desperate cry for attention. Depressive illnesses involve an imbalance of chemicals in the nervous system, and doctors use drugs to try to correct the balance. They may be triggered or caused by outside pressures or strains. This kind of depression is not the same as the normal ups and downs of growing up, nor is it the mild depression most of us feel if we have been let down badly or things have gone wrong.

● **Self-sacrifice** Captain Oates's suicide was for this reason. He was suffering from frostbite, and was therefore slowing down the whole of Scott's party on their return to the ship from the South Pole. He walked out into a blizzard so that the rest of the party could continue at normal speed. Sometimes this is called 'altruistic suicide', because one's life is given on behalf of others.

There are other kinds of altruistic suicide: for example, when the wife of a Hindu was at one time burned on her husband's funeral pyre, or when the Japanese decide upon death rather than dishonour (*hara kiri*).

'The most selfish of crimes'?

Suicide has not been a crime in England since 1963, but it is still a crime to *help* someone to commit suicide.

Is it a selfish thing to do? Would fewer people attempt it if they thought through the consequences? Those left behind have the sorrow of bereavement, but they probably also feel guilty—could they have done something to prevent the tragedy? Should they have seen the warning signs earlier?

There may also be financial worries. Insurance companies, which would pay out when a person dies naturally (on life assurance policies, etc), do not always do so if death has come about through suicide.

Religious attitudes to suicide

Most religions regard suicide as a sin—an offence against God—and something you have to pay for after you die in some way or other. The person who commits it has to answer to God.

● **Muslims** believe that God sent man into the world for a purpose—a man's life is a trust from God. God cannot forgive suicide because it involves running away from life and is a betrayal of the trust.

● **Hindus** believe that you can be forgiven for anything except suicide. They believe that God is everywhere,

MASADA

The rocky cliff-top fortress of Masada, on the western shore of the Dead Sea, was the site of the ritual suicide of 953 Jewish 'freedom-fighters' (Zealots) and their families in AD 73. Despite suicide being forbidden to the Jews, the Zealots chose what they called 'an honourable death' rather than 'fall alive into the hands of the Romans'.

King Herod the Great had turned the huge rock outcrop into a virtually impregnable palace fortress. In AD 66, a party of Zealots captured Masada from the Roman garrison which had occupied it since Herod's death. They adapted the palaces as 'living accommodation' and command posts. After the Romans' destruction of Jerusalem in AD 70, Masada became the last rebel stronghold.

Not until AD 72 did the Romans attempt to retake the fortress: they built a siege wall and a huge assault ramp, finally breaching the walls in AD 73. But rather than surrender, the Zealots burned their belongings and chose ten men to kill every family until all 960 were dead—apart from two women and five children, who escaped by hiding in a cave.

On the last night, the Jewish leader, El'azar, spoke to the rebels:

'My loyal followers, long ago we resolved to serve neither the Romans nor anyone else, but only God, who alone is the true and righteous Lord of men. Now the time has come that bids us prove our determination by our deeds . . . it is evident that daybreak will end our resistance, but we are free

to choose an honourable death with our loved ones . . . After all, we were born to die . . . This even the luckiest man must face. But outrage, slavery and the sight of our wives led away to shame with our children—these are not evils to which man is subject by the laws of nature; men undergo them through their own cowardice if they have a chance to forestall them by death and will not take it . . . Come! While our hands are free and can hold a sword, let them do a noble service! Let us die unenslaved by our enemies, and leave this world as free men in company with our wives and children.'

in everything, so God is actually within and part of the human body. To destroy oneself is therefore an attempt to destroy God. Hindus also believe that their present life is a result of a previous life they have lived. To attempt to escape from life is to attempt to escape from one's destiny.

● Suicide is forbidden to the **Jews**. To them, even self-sacrifice is breaking God's law.

● **Christians** oppose suicide and believe it is wrong (see 'What the Bible says'). And they look to God's mercy and love in cases of illness or impossible pressure which take away people's responsibility. Because of the example of Jesus, they do not oppose self-sacrifice.

The befrienders

Everyone needs friends: people to talk to, give to, relate to and share interests with. The lack of friends and resulting loneliness is the root cause of many suicides.

Chad Varah, a London vicar, came to realize this in 1953. He was very concerned about the number of people in London who were taking their own lives. He set up a telephone answering service and advertised the number of his church so that people in need could phone up and talk. There was no one else for many people to talk to—the police looked upon suicide as a crime and hospitals could not help until the attempt had been made.

Many people in Varah's church became involved as an increasing number of calls were received. A year later, there was so great a demand that the church members decided to set up a small organization. They called themselves 'The Samaritans'.

The Samaritans decided on some basic principles for their work which they have followed ever since:

● It was to be a 'lay movement' and not a professional one. Members could give friendly advice, but if a caller needed help from a doctor, minister, psychiatrist or social worker, the Samaritan was to put them in touch with a professional.

● No Samaritan was allowed to preach or try to convert people in need.

● Helpers would not be barred on grounds of age, sex, colour, creed or politics.

● It was to be for talking and not for the giving of financial help.

● The telephone service was to be available for 24 hours a day, because people might need help at any time.

Figures for the UK show that there is one phone call from about one person in every 250 each year. The calls are mainly from those who are suicidal because, although the Samaritans will give help on other problems, their main aim is to talk to people and so prevent suicide. The suicide rate in Britain was at a peak of 5,714 in 1963. It had dropped to 2,692 by 1979 and the figures have remained at a steady minimal level in all parts of the United Kingdom except Northern Ireland. Because the UK was the only country where a drop took place, many people attributed this to the work of the Samaritans.

UNIT 6

ADDICTION

The use and abuse of drugs have been well known since ancient times. Certain plants were known to have properties which eased pain and cured illnesses.

One of the developments of modern medicine is that these properties have been identified, and in many cases have been mass produced as drugs by industrial chemistry. Other drugs have been developed through an increased understanding of how the body works: for example, streptomycin ended tuberculosis (TB) as a killer disease, and penicillin conquered many types of infection. Used in the right way, drugs are of great value.

It is also possible to *misuse* drugs in a number of ways: taking drugs which have been prescribed for someone else or taking a larger dose than prescribed. But *drug abuse* normally refers to something quite different—taking drugs when there is no need (for health reasons) to take them. They might be taken because they produce some desired mental effect, or to stimulate the body so that it will perform better.

When people talk about 'the drug problem', they are usually referring to this kind of misuse. There are a number of problems associated with it:

● **Habituation** To get the same effect, increasing amounts of the drug have to be taken, because the body gets used to it.

● **Psychological dependence** This is the belief held by a person that he cannot work or think properly unless he has the drug.

● **Physical dependence** This occurs when the body becomes so dependent on the drug that it will not function properly without it. If the drug is not available, the person suffers extremely unpleasant 'withdrawal symptoms'. When someone is physically dependent on a drug, they are known as being 'addicted'.

● **Permanent damage** As the dose of the drug is increased because of habituation, and as the drug is used over a long period because of psychological and physical dependence, the addict often suffers physical and mental damage, which can sometimes result in death.

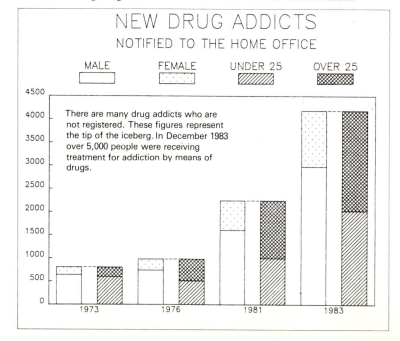

NEW DRUG ADDICTS
NOTIFIED TO THE HOME OFFICE

MALE FEMALE UNDER 25 OVER 25

There are many drug addicts who are not registered. These figures represent the tip of the iceberg. In December 1983 over 5,000 people were receiving treatment for addiction by means of drugs.

1973 1976 1981 1983

The effect of drugs

The table shows the physical and psychological effects of the major types of drugs. There are also far-reaching social consequences:

● Drug-taking makes a person irritable, affecting relationships with family and friends.

● An addict finds it hard to concentrate and may lose his job.

● In desperation, an addict may turn to crime to obtain money for the next dose.

● Taking certain drugs is illegal and conviction leads to a prison sentence.

Why do people take drugs?

Despite the known dangers of drug-taking, misuse appears to be on the increase. There are several reasons why people take drugs:

SOLVENT ABUSE

Solvent sniffing is related to drug abuse and has only recently become a problem among young people—particularly boys in their early teens. It refers to the use of solvents in glues etc to achieve a state of altered awareness, brought about by the chemicals present in these substances.

Solvents are used in this way by young people who are under-age for the legal purchase of alcohol, because most of them have an effect similar to getting drunk. There are many undesirable side-effects: rashes and sores, sleeplessness and nightmares, thirst, permanent colds, depression, inability to work and loss of appetite. Deaths have occurred due to suffocation or vomiting.

● **Desirable effect** People like the immediate effect of the drug so much that they forget about the long-term dangers. An athlete who wants to perform better or a student who wants to stay awake to revise all

❝ I didn't have to go to jail, get stabbed, have all these scars and trips to hospital and a million other things just for the experience! I didn't need six years for the experience. I don't need that kind of life. ❞
Twenty-two-year-old ex-drug addict

night may take amphetamines. Someone wanting relief from tension may take barbiturates.

● **Social pressure** If you are in a group of people experimenting with drugs, it is difficult to resist the pressure to join in. Some of the

DRUG	EFFECT	HAB.	PSY.	PHY.	OTHER EFFECTS
Narcotics					
opium	pain-killers; feeling of well-being and power	√	√	√	withdrawal leads to anxiety and depression; addiction leads to severe illness
morphine		√	√	√	
heroin		√	√	√	
cocaine	euphoria and alertness	√	√	×	irritability, hallucinations; withdrawal causes severe depression
Stimulants					
amphetamines	increased physical performance, gaiety and self-confidence	√	√	×	tension, twitching, high blood pressure and temporary insanity
nicotine	stimulant; calming effect	√	√	×	cancer, heart disease, blood pressure, bronchitis, emphysema
caffeine	stimulant	√̷	√	×	sleeplessness
Depressants					
barbiturates	allay anxiety, give sleep, relax nerves	√	√	√	withdrawal causes anxiety, weakness, temporary insanity
alcohol	decreases anxiety and relaxes inhibitions; loss of judgement, co-ordination and emotional control; sleep	√	√	√	damage to liver, brain cells and stomach lining; excess dosage leads to coma and death
Hallucinogens					
LSD	increased awareness and change of perception; incredible colour images	√̷	√̷	×	loss of reality leads to rash acts; bad images lead to panic; effects sometimes permanent
mescalin		√̷	√̷	×	
cannabis	increases sensory perception, feeling of well-being; change of time sense; sleep	√̷	×	×	no known harm

Key:
Hab. = habituation   √ = Yes   Phy. = physical dependence   × = No
Psy. = psychological dependence   √̷ = Slight or possible

pressure is exerted by 'pushers' who encourage others to take drugs: the money which they receive from addicts provides the drugs for their own use too.

● **'Dropping out'** Some people object to the kind of society in which they live—they see no way to change it or escape from it. They therefore decide to 'drop out' and adopt an alternative life-style. Part of this withdrawal is often achieved by losing consciousness of the society with the aid of drugs. The hippy culture of the 1960s used drugs in this way.

● **Religious experience** Some people claim that drugs can be taken to produce a kind of religious experience. They say that the sense of peace and well-being is the same thing as being in communion with God, although of course chemicals can only react with what is already 'inside you', not giving knowledge but heightening experience or giving new 'unprogrammed' effects as they react with the nervous system and the brain.

Legal drugs?

Alcohol (in beers, wines and spirits) and nicotine (in tobacco) both do much more harm than cannabis, which is an illegal drug! They are so commonly used that they are probably not regarded as 'drugs' at all.

What alcohol is

The correct name for alcohol is ethyl alcohol. It is a chemical which is useful as a fuel, a drying agent and a solvent. Alcohol is present in a wide range of drinks:

4–7% in beer, lager, stout   10–12% in wine

15–22% in port and sherry   40–50% in spirits and liqueurs

The alcohol is present because of the way the drink is made. With wine, yeast cells on the skins of the grapes, or else added to the grape juice, convert the natural sugar into alcohol. When beer is made, the grain is allowed to grow until part of its starch has been naturally converted into sugar. Yeast is then mixed with water, added to the mixture, and again the sugar is converted into alcohol.

This process will produce only about 14 per cent alcohol. Additional alcohol can be added to the drink to heighten its effect. It is also possible to boil the liquid so that the alcohol (and some water) evaporates off. The vapour can then be collected and condensed—this contains much more alcohol than the original liquid while still retaining its flavour.

What alcohol does

Alcohol always has a very quick effect, because it passes straight through the wall of the stomach into the bloodstream and is rapidly conveyed to every cell in the body. It can seriously damage the stomach wall by causing gastritis and ulcers; because it is a poison, it can ultimately cause coma and death.

Absorbed into the bloodstream, alcohol has a number of effects on the human body:

● Alcohol makes the red blood cells stick together. This affects the oxygen-carrying capacity of the blood, so that **circulation slows down**. The brain cells begin to starve because of lack of oxygen. There is a loss of control over movement, slurred speech, inability to focus the eye and poor judgement.

● Alcohol **slows down the work of the body cells**. The liver tries to get rid of the alcohol by converting it into sugar, which can be easily removed from the body. But to do this, it needs additional oxygen, which is not available due to the effect of the alcohol on the red blood cells. The liver cells begin to die; if this process continues unchecked, a fatal disease called cirrhosis develops.

● Alcohol **affects the 'censor' mechanism of the brain**. Control of our basic instincts such as sex, aggression and crude speech, is kept by the censor mechanism. Alcohol stops the mechanism from working so that we become less inhibited. Unfortunately, the effect does not stop just at 'getting the party going': as more alcohol is taken, people become more aggressive, talk loudly and may become sexually offensive.

● Alcohol **affects the health of the next generation** because it can damage the unborn child. The child of a woman who drinks a lot is generally undersized and sometimes mentally deficient. Over a measured period of time in a New York hospital, 83 per cent of children born to women who were addicted to alcohol were born with deformities. Pregnant women are advised to drink

'Has the Government got it wrong?'

	Government expenditure against		
	Drugs	Alcohol	Tobacco
User deaths per year	235	7,700	100,000
Expenditure by Government	£411 million	£2.65 million	£3.5 million
Money spent per death	£1.7 million	£344	£35

In 1983 the University of York did a study to calculate the cost of alcohol abuse. It was concluded that it cost the UK a staggering £1,680 million per year. Some of the accounts are as follows:

	£ million
sickness absence from work	641.51
unemployment	144.74
premature death	567.70
hospital treatment	25.77
illnesses related to alcohol	68.58
damage in road accidents	89.20
costs in court	15.79

very little alcohol or to give it up altogether.

● Alcohol is **addictive**. It makes people psychologically dependent— they believe they cannot be sociable at a party or do a job properly without a drink. Alcohol also makes people physically dependent, because if the body is denied alcohol after a certain stage is reached, there are severe withdrawal symptoms (similar to withdrawal from hard drugs) such as trembling, sickness, depression and even mental delusions. Alcohol also causes habituation: more and more is required to produce the same effect.

'Wider still and wider'

Apart from its damaging effect on health (usually, but not exclusively, that of the person drinking it), alcohol is responsible for a wide range of social problems.

In addition to such costs, alcohol often costs suffering and embarrassment through lack of self control, the break-up of families and friendships and problems with working relationships.

Attitudes in world faiths

Religious groups have different approaches to the use of alcohol.

The Qur'an forbids alcohol, because it destroys health, the pocket and reason. However, there is a difference of practice in some Muslim countries. For example, Jordan allows alcohol and it is used by the armed forces, but in other countries, there are severe penalties for even handling alcohol.

The Hindu believes that both drugs and alcohol lead to darkness; they blind logic and discrimination and ruin friendships, and should therefore be avoided.

Alcohol is often mentioned in the Jewish scriptures. These teach that alcohol should be used with care and in moderation, but not prohibited. Wine is always drunk at the Jewish Festival of Passover.

Christians have varied in their approach. There have always been those who believe that Christians should be teetotallers, i.e. total abstainers. Other Christians take the view that alcohol should be used sensibly and sparingly.

Jesus obviously drank wine: he turned 120 gallons of water used for ritual purification into wine at a wedding—to point up the fact that his kingdom was to be like the taste

'THAT'S THE WAY THE MONEY GOES'

Consumer spending in UK in 1983 (millions of pounds)

food	£27,148	fuel and power	£9,395	alcohol	£13,372
housing	£27,326	household goods		tobacco	£6,208
clothing	£12,114	and services	£12,274	transport	
		post and telephone	£3,206	(buying and running car; public transport)	£28,269

? What do you notice about spending patterns?

? Why might alcohol cause 'secondary poverty'?

? What social problems could this lead to?

Percentage of income spent in UK

	1977	1979	1981	1983
alcohol	7.6	7.3	7.3	7.3
tobacco	4.2	3.6	3.6	3.4
food	18.5	17.3	15.9	14.9
housing	13.4	13.2	14.8	15.0
clothing	7.7	7.8	6.7	6.6
household goods and services	7.3	7.7	6.9	6.7
transport	14.6	16.1	16.5	17.3
other goods	12.6	13.3	13.9	14.6

? On which items has expenditure increased?

? Are they costs which we can control or not?

? Why do you think that alcohol consumption has increased?

? Why do you think that spending on tobacco has decreased?

ALCOHOLICS ANONYMOUS

There are said to be over 500,000 alcoholics (that is, people *addicted* to alcohol) in the UK. In Liverpool alone, there are known to be over 3,000—a number which includes housewives, labourers, teachers and doctors.

Because of the devastating effects of alcohol on individual, family and national life, organizations have been founded to help those who want to break the habit. One of the most well known is Alcoholics Anonymous (AA), founded in 1935 by a New York stockbroker and an Ohio surgeon. These two men were both addicted to alcohol. They believed that they could help one another if they faced up to their situation and involved themselves with others who also wanted to get over their drink problem.

AA is now an international organization with 28,000 groups of recovered alcoholics in ninety-two countries. Each group tries to help other alcoholics to break the habit. Part of the help comes through local meetings at which speakers may recount how they got over their addiction, and the AA programme is explained. People are encouraged to give up drinking for one day at a time.

The philosophy of Alcoholics Anonymous is conveyed through the 'Twelve Steps' which the founders discovered they had to follow in order to break their addiction to alcohol. The first three steps say:

● We admit we are powerless over alcohol—that our lives have become unmanageable.
● We have come to believe that a power greater than ourselves can restore us.
● We have made a decision to turn our wills and our lives over to the care of God as we understand him.

The organization's Christian basis is seen in these steps, although AA is open to anyone of any faith who needs help.

? Why do you think AA has been able to help so many people to be cured of alcoholism?
? Why is it helpful to be 'anonymous'?
? Do you think that a faith in God would help someone to conquer alcohol addiction?

of wine after water! On another occasion, he was criticized by the Pharisees for drinking. The apostle Paul encouraged Timothy to use wine as a medicine. It is abuse rather than use which seems to be wrong, and therefore the Bible condemns drunkenness.

No smoke without fire?

Christopher Columbus was the first European to see people smoking the leaves of the tobacco plant in 1492. It was brought to England by Sir Francis Drake and Sir Walter Raleigh in the sixteenth century.

There are about 1,000 constituents of tobacco. One of these, nicotine, is so habit-forming that when a person is addicted, the other constituents become harmful too. As well as being addictive, nicotine is known to be a major cause of heart disease and thrombosis; tobacco also contains carcinogens, which cause cancer of the mouth, throat and lungs. Most of the 36,000 people who die in the UK each year from lung cancer have been habitual smokers. There are other irritants in the smoke which cause problems for the eyes, nose and throat, but the greatest irritation is set up in the lungs, where the smoke causes bronchitis, asthma and emphysema. In the UK, 30,000 people die each year from bronchitis—and a smoker is twenty-five times more likely to get bronchitis than a non-smoker.

When tobacco is burned, carbon monoxide is given off. This is a poisonous gas which combines with the red blood cells so that they cannot absorb oxygen. This causes oxygen starvation, and the cells are killed, resulting in breathlessness and high blood pressure. In addition to this, smoking destroys the sense of taste. Seldom can a substance have brought so much misery!

Smoking affects other people besides the smoker:

● Carbon monoxide affects the blood of non-smokers who are in a smoke-filled room and they are subject to the cancer-producing substances too: an hour in a smoke-filled room is the equivalent of smoking one cigarette.
● Unborn babies are affected by nicotine. It is generally thought that

smoking has an adverse effect on the blood supply to the uterus and reduces the oxygen supply to the baby. If a woman smokes during pregnancy, her baby may be underweight at birth. Babies of heavy smokers (thirty cigarettes a day or more) almost certainly will suffer physical and mental retardation in later childhood.

● Smoking is a fire hazard. In 1983, 396 people died in fires in the home and it is believed that a high proportion of these were due to smoking.
● Tobacco is also a factor in secondary poverty. Cigarettes can be a major part of the family budget for a heavy smoker.

Why do people smoke?

People rarely start to smoke because they enjoy it—the first smoke is normally very unpleasant! So why *do* they smoke? The main reasons seem to come down to social pressures of various kinds, and advertising.

Because of the problems caused by smoking, the British government itself, and bodies such as the Health Education Council and Action on Smoking and Health (ASH), use advertising and literature to try to dissuade people from smoking. In the same year as a total of £1 million was spent on such campaigns, the tobacco industry spent £83 million on advertising and one company alone made £250 million profit.

A CHRISTIAN VIEW

Christians in the Methodist Church have formulated a statement which summarizes the Christian attitude to drugs, alcohol and tobacco:

'The Christian's faith teaches him to use all things, including his money, responsibly. He seeks to meet problems and stresses by following Christ's teaching and living by his power. To Christ he offers the undiminished vigour of his body and mind. He loves his neighbour and therefore examines the probable effect of his behaviour, his habits and his example upon his neighbour. He accepts his part in the responsibility of the Church in the way of education and rehabilitation.'

Christians might differ on details, but they would agree on the following broad principles:
● For a Christian, the body is where God's Spirit lives and should be treated with respect.
● A Christian wants to be under Jesus Christ's control, not controlled by some harmful substance.
● A secure relationship with God gives the feeling of worth and acceptance that some people seek by taking drugs, by drinking or smoking.
● In difficult or pressured situations, God's strength and help are available.

● Powerful advertising portrays smoking as adult, socially acceptable and glamorous, and sport sponsorship gives 'free' advertising every time the particular competition is mentioned and promotes the image that sportsmen are smokers.
● Young people may begin smoking as a protest/sign of independence/bid to be regarded as adult.
● There is pressure to conform to group behaviour.
● Smoking relieves tension and helps some people become relaxed and calm when they are under pressure of some kind.

Once someone has started to smoke, however, they are faced with the problems associated with other 'drugs' listed at the beginning of this chapter: habituation (more and more cigarettes are needed), physical and psychological dependence.

Discussion topics

1 With drug-taking, drinking and smoking, can you honestly say 'Why shouldn't I? It's only me that suffers!' (Think as widely as possible.)

2 The government earns a lot of revenue from the high taxes on alcohol and tobacco, at the same time as warning us of their dangers. Is their attitude realistic or two-faced?

3 List as many sporting events as you can think of which are sponsored by tobacco companies. Do you think this is right?

4 Look back at the second table on consumer spending patterns. What has happened to spending on tobacco in the UK? This is true for many countries in the Western world. Tobacco companies are therefore conducting big sales campaigns in Third World countries. Do you think this is morally right?

5 When grain is used to make beer, 70 per cent of its food value is lost. In a world where millions are starving, should a basic foodstuff be used to manufacture something positively harmful?

6 Do you think the Christian view on drugs, drink and smoking is sensible/practical/restricting/unrealistic?

7 Do you think that glue-sniffing is dangerous?

MONEY

Before the development of money, society operated a system of barter: for example, in a village where everyone grew their own crops, a bag of potatoes might be exchanged for a bag of carrots, or four bales of hay for two gallons of milk, according to what people needed.

As society became more complex, another system evolved. The potatoes, carrots, hay and milk gradually came to be exchanged for something quite different (an agreed amount of metal, in each case) which people could then use to exchange for other items they wanted. Metal was found to be the most useful material for this purpose, because it lasted. The system worked, provided that everyone accepted the value of certain weights of metal.

The weighing of metal was a better system than barter, although the two existed side by side for a long time. However, it was still not very convenient. Metal came in all shapes, sizes, weights and states of purity, so it was necessary to have scales or a balance to weigh the metal every time an exchange was made.

The idea of coinage, or money, probably first came into being in the seventh century BC. Coins were small pieces of metal of standard weight and purity; someone in authority (normally the king) put his mark (or 'seal') on the metal to guarantee both. The most useful shape for a coin was a disc. The names of the weights which had previously been used to weigh out the metal were transferred to the first coins. A shekel weight therefore became a 'shekel', and it weighed just over 11gm/0.39oz.

The coins used in the UK had a much later origin. It was in AD 760 that King Offa of Mercia declared that a 'pound' was a pound of pure silver. It was to be divided into twenty silver shillings and 240 silver pence.

Money as a symbol

When William of Normandy became king of England in 1066, he devalued the coinage. He reduced the weight of the silver in a pound by 6 per cent and reduced the purity of the silver by 10 per cent. In one sense this did not matter, because although there was no longer a pound's-worth (weight) of silver, it stood for a pound's-worth of silver, so it could be used to buy the same quantity of goods or services. In the fifteenth century, Henry VIII devalued the coinage several times. By this time, everyone accepted the coin as a symbol: it was worth what people said it was worth.

This is how we regard money today. A ten-pound note is worth very little in terms of actual paper and print, but because everybody accepts the value which is printed on it, it can be used to pay for ten pounds'-worth of goods or services. If there is sufficient confidence in the value of the symbol, then this system of money works.

More recently, the use of other kinds of money has become widespread: trading stamps, telephone stamps, record tokens, postal orders, cheques and credit cards can all be used instead of coins and notes. Stamps and tokens are very similar to money, but cheques and credit cards differ. A cheque can be used to transfer money from my bank to the bank where someone else keeps their money (has an account). No money physically changes hands, but the cheque authorizes the deduction of the sum I have written from my account, and its addition to the account of the person to whom I owe money. A credit card guarantees a trader that a finance company will pay him what is owed, because the company has agreed with me that I will repay them every month.

? What are the advantages of using cheques and credit cards as methods of payment?

? Can you think of any disadvantages?

'Going up'

You always seem to need more money to pay for a car this year than you did, say, three years ago, and the cost of food items often varies from week to week. The familiar cry, 'Prices have gone up again', is another way of saying, 'Our money is worth less'. When goods and services continue to cost more because our money is worth less, then we are experiencing 'inflation'.

Economists do not agree on the causes of, or solutions to, inflation. The reasons for it are many and complex. Here are two possible explanations:

● Inflation occurs **when demand is greater than supply**. Suppliers know that people will pay more for certain goods, because there is competition to purchase them. They therefore allow the prices to rise.

● Inflation occurs **when there is too much money in circulation**. If people have twice as much money as is needed to buy the goods they want, then prices will increase to the point where the surplus money is absorbed. It is quite easy for this to happen when a coin or note is simply a symbol, because a government can print or mint as much money as it requires, but by doing so it brings about an increase in prices. This is why it is said that if wages rise without an increase in the goods available (productivity), then there will be higher inflation.

Money, money, money

Money is obviously of great importance—without a means of exchange, modern society would cease to function. Money provides us with the necessities of life (food, clothing, warmth and shelter) and maybe with some luxuries as well. Paid employment is the means by which most people obtain the money they need. In the UK, if you are unable to work, the government guarantees to pay you a certain basic minimum to try to cover basic necessities.

Apart from working for it, there are several other ways of obtaining money:

● **Borrowing** This may be on a friendly, informal basis, but usually, if large sums are involved, money is borrowed from a bank, building society or insurance company, and has to be paid back with interest. Buying goods with credit cards or on a hire purchase agreement is another (expensive) way of borrowing money, and interest is charged on these loans too.

? What are the advantages and disadvantages of buying something this way?

MAKING ENDS MEET

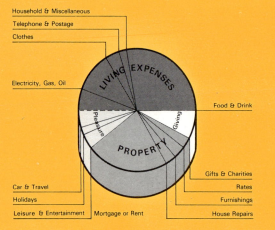

Household & Miscellaneous
Telephone & Postage
Clothes
Electricity, Gas, Oil
LIVING EXPENSES
Pleasure
Giving
PROPERTY
Food & Drink
Car & Travel
Holidays
Leisure & Entertainment
Mortgage or Rent
Gifts & Charities
Rates
Furnishings
House Repairs

? For your own 'income' (allowance, pocket money, part-time or holiday earnings), devise a similar chart to show how you spend your money.

? Is your spending all on yourself or do you consider other people's needs?

● **Taking** This may take the very obvious form of stealing (illegal) or may be by more subtle exploitation and oppression of those who are poor and weak. In ancient times, it was the practice to demand 'protection money' from weaker states if they wished to avoid conquest, and to demand taxes when conquest took place!

? Are modern-day tariff-barriers a way of richer countries taking money from poorer, developing countries?

● **Investment** It would be hard for modern business to exist without the investment of other people's money. An investor (an individual or organization) puts his money to work and receives a proportion of the profits made by the concern he chooses to lend his money to. This may be by putting savings into an account in the local building society or by buying shares in a commercial company.

? What questions would you ask before you invested money in something?

● **Gambling** A risk is taken with a certain amount of money in the hope of 'making a killing', i.e. winning a much greater amount of money. This is such a significant means of obtaining (and losing!) money that we are going to look at it in more detail.

The luck of the draw

Many people pay money each week to the football pools' promoters in the hope of winning a fortune.

Smaller sums are won by people who take part in lotteries, raffles, prize bingo or who put a few pence each way on a horse. There is something exciting about the element of chance and the prospect of winning that gives gambling its appeal. And why not?

A gamble is defined as: 'A transaction between two parties, whereby the transfer of something of value is made dependent upon chance in such a way that the gain of one party equals the whole loss of the other.' Card games may contain elements of chance, but only constitute gambling if stakes are played for. Tossing a coin is an appeal to chance but hardly a gamble in that sense of the word.

Some Jewish leaders have approved gambling; others have condemned it. Those in favour point out that dice games were very popular in the ancient world, and that neither dice games nor any other gambles were condemned by the law. Dice were actually used to reveal·God's will: it was believed that God was so completely in control of everything that happened in the world, that even the throw of a dice was in his power. If a fortune was made, then the fortune was God's will and God's gift. Those who disapproved believed that gambling showed a lack of faith

'Today's spectator is tomorrow's gambler.' The attraction of gambling is very strong. One win can get you hooked! It can become an addiction like drugs or alcohol.

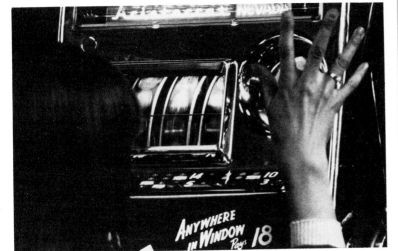

WHAT THE BIBLE SAYS ABOUT WEALTH

[God says] ' ''For the world and everything in it is mine.'' ' (Psalm 50:12)

'If God gives a man wealth and property and lets him enjoy them, he should be grateful and enjoy what he has worked for.' (Ecclesiastes 5:19)
Money and possessions are gifts from God. They ultimately belong to him and should be used wisely and carefully because they are 'on trust' from the true owner. ·

★ ★ ★

'If you love money, you will never be satisfied; if you long to be rich, you will never get all you want . . . It is better to be satisfied with what you have than to be always wanting something else.' (Ecclesiastes 5:10, 6:9)
Seeking after wealth leads to dissatisfaction and discontent.

★ ★ ★

[Jesus said] ' ''A person's true life is not made up of the things he owns, no matter how rich he may be.'' ' (Luke 12:15)
Wealth is not what life is all about —there are far more important concerns. It should not be the standard by which we judge other people. The temptation to be greedy and selfish should be resisted.

★ ★ ★

'Each one should give, then, as he has decided, not with regret or out of a sense of duty; for God loves the one who gives gladly. And God is able to give you more than you need, so that you will always have all you need for yourselves and more than enough for every good cause.' (2 Corinthians 9:7–8)
A Christian should be thankful to God for supplying his needs, and generous in using his money to meet the needs of others.

in God: trying to 'get rich quick' instead of trusting God for one's daily needs.

There is a similarly wide difference of view among Christians today. The Roman Catholic Church looks upon gambling as a luxury rather than a sin—there is no harm in it provided all other commitments have been met. Other Christians are strongly opposed to gambling. The Methodist Church considers that it is 'so great an evil' that no Christian should have anything to do with it. Their reasoning runs as follows:

● Gambling transfers money from one person to another entirely by chance. This is wrong because it leaves dependence on God's care out of the situation.
● The money gained is made entirely at the expense of another person, and this is not 'loving your neighbour'.
● Something of value is gained without giving any goods or services in exchange, and this is irresponsible business practice.
● Gambling ruins sport.
● Gambling puts society at risk because it causes crime and poverty, and because the thought of getting rich quickly takes away the will to work.

Other Christians give further reasons for their opposition to gambling:
● It becomes a habit which many people cannot afford.
● It brings misery and can destroy people when it gets out of control.
● It is against common sense because the odds are always against a win.
● It is an irresponsible use of the money which God has entrusted to us.
● It denies the Christian belief that Jesus brings complete satisfaction in life.
● It encourages greed and selfishness.
● It thrives on chance, in direct contrast to the character of the God of the Bible—a God of order.

Servant or master?

Money has been said to be a good servant, but a bad master. Kept in its right place, used as a means of exchange and a way of helping

others, it is very valuable indeed. But when it becomes a way by which we evaluate life itself, by which we judge other people, it becomes very dangerous. When money becomes a reason for oppressing others, and even *a means of* oppressing others, it is true to say (as the Bible does) that the love of money (not money itself) is the root of all evil.

Jesus made three very important observations about money in the Sermon on the Mount:
● Money decays (Matthew 6:19–20)
● Money distorts (Matthew 6:21–23)
● Money divides (Matthew 6:24)
● **Money decays** It does not last, and we can lose it. 'You can't take it with you' is an old but true saying.
● **Money distorts** It can twist our view of reality and warp our sense of values. Getting money becomes the most important aim in life to the exclusion of everything else, including other people's needs.
● **Money divides** It causes inequalities and therefore divisions between man and man. It divides man from God as well, because God hates injustice; also, people who spend all their time and effort getting money will have little time for God.

Although money is valuable—valuable enough to work for it and to save it—it is not all *that* valuable. It certainly is not the most important thing in life. Money cannot buy peace of mind, happiness, friendship or a right relationship with God.

Discussion topics

1 Why are some of the richest people unhappy?

2 Would you agree with someone who said, 'I can do what I like with my money'?

3 Do you think that the division between rich and poor countries in the world is just greed and selfishness on a global scale?

4 Do you think it is OK to buy goods on credit?

5 Which of the following views on gambling would you support and why:
● 'All gambling is wrong.'
● 'It's only a bit of fun. Everyone has a flutter now and then.'
● 'But the money's going to a good cause.'

UNIT 8

LEISURE

Leisure is very difficult to define. If a person's job is dull, repetitive or boring, almost anything done when work is over is enjoyable! 'Leisure' has therefore come to be associated with 'pleasure'—i.e. the pleasurable things one can do once work is finished.

But this view of leisure has certain problems. When teachers take a class on a geography field trip, they will often enjoy it as much as a day out. Work can be pleasurable! When a builder decides to put an extension on his own house at the end of a working day and at week-ends, he is doing the same thing as at work, but it is his 'leisure time'. Are those activities work or leisure? And if we talk about leisure as distinct from 'paid employment', what happens to leisure time for housewives or students?

Or is leisure to be seen as rest and relaxation? Surely those are elements of it—but some people are vigorously energetic in their leisure activities, exerting themselves far more than their job demands!

Leisure's association with pleasure has given it a 'bad press' among some people who claim to find support from the Bible that the only rest from work should be on a Sunday so as to worship God, or that pleasure itself is wrong. Both these extreme views emphasize long hours of hard work with no recreation or leisure whatsoever and, in doing so, misrepresent the balanced teaching of the Bible.

The importance of leisure

Leisure activity is a very important aspect of modern society for a number of reasons:
● **Leisure time is increasing** It was not so long ago that everyone in

the family worked all the daylight hours, and when work was over, they slept. Gradually the working week has become shorter and the number of annual days' holiday has increased. Micro-chip technology is already releasing people from dull and repetitive work, and could mean that fewer full-time jobs will be available in the future, although the new technology creates many new jobs as well, as happened in the Industrial Revolution.

For some people, leisure time has been increased through unemployment. It is therefore important to consider leisure because the time available for it is, in general, on the increase.

● **Leisure prepares us for life**
One form of leisure activity associated with children is 'play'. When children play together, they learn how to get on with others, how to react when things appear unfair, what can be said and what cannot, what is expected of them in a group. 'Play activity' has value at every age—some sports enjoyed by adults may well teach perseverance, patience and team spirit.

● **Leisure enables us to work better** The saying 'All work and no play makes Jack a dull boy'

originated at a time when children used to work all day in the mills or mines. They got more and more tired, and became dull and listless in their work. Fortunately, social conditions have changed, but it is now widely accepted that leisure time is necessary for people to 'recharge their batteries'—to regain their strength and energy. The working men's clubs in areas of heavy industry give the men a chance to recover from their work; the hard-pressed executive can cope with a long working day if he relaxes by playing an energetic game of squash.

This is one of the reasons why organizations such as the Lord's Day Observance Society protest against Sunday activities—not to be killjoys, but to protect those whose needed leisure time would be eroded by having to work on their 'day off'.

● **Leisure has become an industry** As people work shorter hours, and more money is available

to purchase more than just necessities, a large industry has grown up to meet leisure needs. These may be 'passive' leisure pursuits—such as watching television, going to a soccer match or to the theatre—or 'active' pursuits: cycling, reading, sport or going to a disco. There is also a whole branch of the leisure industry catering for holidays, travel and tourism. Millions of pounds are spent on these activities every year, and they provide employment for large numbers of people.

Leisure is a question of balance, never of just 'filling in time'. Someone who sits at a desk all week should take up a strenuous physical activity; someone who spends their day working at a machine should get involved with people in their leisure time; someone whose work makes them tense needs a leisure activity which is calm and uninterrupted.

● **Leisure leads to social integration** Imagine moving to live on a new estate. During the day you are at work. How are you going to get to know your new neighbours? How are you going to make friends? It will be through leisure activities. Mothers will have coffee together after taking their children to playgroup or school; teenagers may meet in the church youth group; sporting enthusiasts join local tennis, football or squash clubs. Gradually newcomers become less isolated and increasingly feel part of the community. Shared leisure activities help to bring about the sense of belonging, or social integration, at various levels.

Leisure and world faiths

Hindus believe that leisure should be used to get to know literature, music and art, and that the knowledge should be purely for pleasure. They also see leisure as an opportunity to become involved in the community and in social work.

Muslims believe that leisure time should be used constructively. Games are learned and played, and there is a lot of work done for charity. There is less professionalism in sport in a Muslim country than is common in the West, and the sexual themes which are part of so much Western entertainment are not nearly so obvious. Many strict Muslims would not listen to pop music or go to the cinema.

In the Bible, God made the 'seventh day' as a day to enter into the results of our work, as a break from it, as 'rest', 're-creation', time for fellowship with God and with others. Christians believe that leisure should balance our work (or normal activity) so that we are 'whole people', i.e. balanced human beings. It should compensate for the things which tend to dehumanize us.

Assignments and discussion topics

1 Could unemployment be described as 'enforced leisure'? Should people be prepared (i.e. 'trained') for it in some way? How can a time of

WHAT THE BIBLE SAYS ABOUT LEISURE

' "You have six days in which to do your work, but the seventh day is a day of rest dedicated to me. On that day no one is to work . . ." ' (Exodus 20:9–10)

'There were so many people coming and going that Jesus and his disciples didn't even have time to eat. So he said to them, "Let us go off by ourselves to some place where we will be alone and you can rest for a while." So they started out in a boat by themselves for a lonely place.' (Mark 6:31–32)

Rest and relaxation are part of God's plan and are needed to balance the time spent working. For Christians, some of their 'leisure' will include time to worship and serve God.

★ ★ ★

'Fill your minds with those things that are good and that deserve praise: things that are true, noble, right, pure, lovely and honourable.' (Philippians 4:8)

The same standards of honesty, purity and fairness should apply to work and leisure alike. Christians will want to avoid leisure pursuits which could damage their relationship with God.

★ ★ ★

'God . . . generously gives us everything for our enjoyment.' (1 Timothy 6:17)

Pleasure is not an end in itself, but use of leisure time should be positively enjoyable.

★ ★ ★

[Jesus said] ' "I have come in order that you might have life—life in all its fullness." ' (John 10:10)

Leisure should contribute to making us whole, balanced people— enjoying 'fullness of life' physically, mentally and spiritually.

unemployment be used for acquiring skills?

2 Do you think all leisure time should be used constructively —for some purposeful activity?

3 Is the prospect of increased leisure time a blessing or a bore to you?

4 Make a list of the things you do each day during a typical week. Then divide them into those that you *have* to do (sleeping, eating, homework . . .) and those that you *choose* to do (watching television, reading, going for a walk . . .) Work out (on average) how much time you spend per day/per week on these two types of activity.

5 Why is it that some spectator sports, which contribute a great deal to leisure, lead to violence of this kind?

On 29 May 1985 Liverpool played Juventus for the European Cup. But the match is remembered for the events on the terraces. Liverpool fans went on a violent rampage, a wall collapsed, and several people were killed.

UNIT 9

SOCIAL RELATIONSHIPS

Every human being is unique. Not only are there physical differences, but also different personality characteristics, different levels of ability, not to mention differences of language, custom or culture. Each person is an important individual in his or her own right, with a contribution to make to life that no one else can make.

A 'social animal'

Although each of us is unique, we cannot live by ourselves. This applies to providing for ourselves, but it goes further than that. If you were in solitary confinement in prison for many years, or if you were cast away on a desert island, you would lose many of the skills which are vital to being human.

Left alone, there would be no need to speak or listen to people, or even to think clearly. You would not need to consider anyone else and so would become completely self-centred. There would be nobody around to stop you becoming inward-looking. If you lost the power of communication, of thinking clearly, of consciousness of other people and of looking beyond yourself, you would have lost a lot of what it means to be human.

In normal life, we fulfil our social needs by forming friendships with other people with whom we have something in common (see Unit 1, Friendship). We may like playing the same sport, have been brought up in the same place, been to school together, or on holiday at the same place and time. We may have come from a similar background or we may worship God in the same kind of way.

Hostility between groups

It is important for a person to feel happy and secure in himself; it is also important to feel happy and secure in a group. When a group of football supporters goes a long distance to support their team at an away match, they sometimes feel anxious at a ground in another town, where everybody seems to be a supporter of the local club. Anxiety of this kind often leads to feelings of hostility, particularly if one group misunderstands the other, or feels that it has been unfairly treated.

There are several groups in our society where there are misunderstandings which give rise on occasion to hostility.

● **Old and young** Today's old people remember their youth as a time of struggle and hardship: housing was poor, money was short and there was less opportunity for education. Social services did not exist, personal possessions were few, there was little entertainment, and if they *did* go out for an evening, they had to be home very early. It seems to them that today's young people have much greater freedom, a lot of money to spend on themselves, lead an active life with plenty of leisure facilities, but are often still discontented.

It is easy for each group to generalize about the other: old people are 'old-fashioned', 'boring', 'past it', 'always going on about the good old days', while young people are 'inconsiderate', 'always listening to that awful pop music', 'don't know what a hard day's work is all about' and 'have more money than is good for them'. Obviously not everyone thinks in these kind of stereotypes, but the possibility of hostility is there.

● **Healthy and handicapped** People who are physically or mentally handicapped often need the support of able-bodied people to help them live a more normal life. Sometimes, however, their very handicap makes healthy people feel insecure so that they do not treat handicapped people as normal human beings. A mentally handicapped person might not be fully aware of his isolation, whereas a physically handicapped person with limbs distorted through disease or a face disfigured by burns is very sensitive to the fact that others want to keep him at a distance.

The 'hostility' between these two groups may show itself in feelings of resentment and bitterness on the part of the handicapped, and guilt, fear and embarrassment on the part of the healthy. The overall result is withdrawal from each other's company.

● **Male and female** In some areas of society, there is hostility between men and women. The traditional view has been that 'a woman's place is in the home', and society has been structured so that by education, training and social conditioning, women were prepared for such a role. Some men have looked upon women more or less as servants who are there to do their bidding.

In their attempts to achieve equal status, women have sometimes found it necessary to take hostile action against men. They have campaigned vigorously for the right to vote, to enter the professions, to join the same clubs and to obtain the same wage for the same work.

Discrimination is sometimes seen in the number of physical attacks on women by men. In the British Crime Survey, of women aged sixteen and over, sixteen in every 10,000 in England and Wales said they had been sexually assaulted. In 1981 the figure was thirty-four in every 10,000 in Scotland. The difference may be due to the fact that police procedures in Scotland may encourage victims to report such offences. This too may be a mark of discrimination.

● **Social class** In Britain, the Registrar General divides people into social classes according to their occupation.

Classes III, IV and V are generally referred to as the 'working class', accounting for 79.4 per cent of the population. In the past, the majority of working-class people worked long hours in poor conditions for low pay, were inadequately housed and received little education. By contrast, the wealthy often lived in large and well-built homes, waited on by servants.

The two extremes have traditionally opposed one another: as shop-floor and management in industry, Labour and Conservative in politics, coming respectively from council estates and privately-owned houses. The lines of demarcation are not so distinct as they used to be, but there is still conflict, especially in the world of work. Social distinctions are also still evident—in housing, education, leisure activities and spending patterns.

● **Colour** There is sometimes hostility between groups of people of a different colour, particularly between blacks and whites. The past has left its mark upon the present: in the past, many whites believed that blacks were inferior to them. They conquered and colonized areas occupied by black races, and exploited black labour—by shipping them away into slavery or by taking over their land, then 'employing' them to work on it for white masters. Many black and coloured people still feel (often justifiably) that they are unfairly treated in a white-dominated society. This leads to insecurity, misunderstanding, resentment and

sometimes open hostility.

● **Race** There can often be feelings of hostility between races, quite apart from the issue of colour. Conflict between tribes, sometimes leading to civil war, has been one of the major problems which has faced many newly-independent African states. Conflict arises because one race looks upon another as inferior, and treats its members accordingly.

Racial prejudice was probably the historical reason for the caste system in the Hindu religion. When the Aryan peoples arrived in India around 1400 BC, it is thought that they may have become the top three

Class	Job description	Examples of jobs
I	Professional	doctor, dentist, university lecturer, engineer
II	Managerial and technical	librarian, teacher, nurse, pharmacist, owner
IIIa	(Non-manual) clerical and minor supervisory	of small business clerk, typist, shop assistant
IIIb	(Manual) skilled trades	driver, electrician, hairdresser, porter, tailor
IV	Semi-skilled work	bus conductor, postman, storekeeper, waiter
V	Unskilled work	labourer, messenger, window cleaner

castes. The original inhabitants then became the fourth caste, or *shudras*, the unskilled labourers. Groups of no definite caste were regarded as 'untouchables' and were banished from society.

● **Religion** Religion does not always unite people. As it is often

what people feel most deeply about, it unfortunately divides people and is the cause of bitter hostility. This was true in the period of the Crusades, when Christians fought Muslims in the mistaken view that they should repossess the Holy Land. In the past, too, Christians have wrongly persecuted Jews because 'Jews were the people who crucified Christ'. Both Protestants and Catholics died for their faith in England at the time of the Reformation. Part of the problem of the continuing conflict in Northern Ireland lies in the mistrust and hostility between Protestant and Catholic: the religions in this case are the 'badge' of people of different origins. Different groups within the Christian church emphasize different facets of the faith and sometimes

South Africa's 'apartheid' policies have led to racial violence. Twenty thousand people attended this funeral of blacks killed by police.

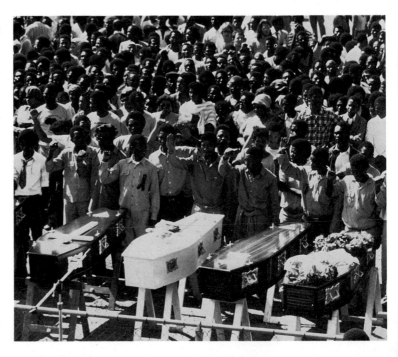

seem to be at odds with each other instead of standing together. Combining nationalism with religion, Muslim states such as Iran have bitterly opposed Western, so-called 'Christian' countries as part of the resurgence of Islam.

Degrees of hostility

Some conflicts do not matter—they are deliberately used in sport, for example. There is a 'conflict' between rival teams in football matches, and provided the keen, competitive spirit is kept under control by the referee and does not erupt into violence on the pitch, it is acceptable and enjoyable.

However, there are other forms of hostility and conflict which are not at all acceptable *or* enjoyable.

● **Prejudice** The term 'prejudice' comes from a Latin word, *praejudicum*. The *praejudicum* was a court in which the rank of parties was established *before* a trial was held. Prejudice has therefore come to mean a preconceived idea or bias about something or someone—i.e. an opinion formed before knowing the truth of the matter. It does not

❝ Prejudice is a great time-saver: you can make up your mind without bothering with facts. ❞

always have to be negative ('Immigrants are taking all our jobs'); it could be positive ('If that cake was made by Jane's mum, it must be good!'). Prejudice does not have to involve people. We can be prejudiced about food if we say we do not like it *before* we have tried it.

Prejudice is an attitude which is 'caught' rather than learned, because learning involves finding out *facts*, leaving no room for prejudice. People become prejudiced because their parents or friends have prejudiced opinions. This often results in derogatory words ('wogs'), insulting jokes ('Have you heard about the Irishman who . . .') and a fixed idea about other nationalities. The idea that all Scots are tight with their money may apply to *some* Scotsmen, but when it is applied to *all* Scotsmen, it becomes a stereotype.

WHAT THE BIBLE SAYS

'Sin came into the world through one man, and his sin brought death with it. As a result, death has spread to the whole human race because everyone has sinned.' (Romans 5:12)

'It is your sins that separate you from God . . . You are guilty of lying, violence, and murder.' (Isaiah 59:2)
The world is spoilt by sin, and it is this which makes for selfishness, divisions and prejudice. The very beginning of the Bible shows how man's disobedience of God ('the Fall') resulted in broken relationships —he was alienated from God and from other people.

'When anyone is joined to Christ, he is a new being; the old is gone, the new has come. All this is done by God, who through Christ changed us from enemies into his friends and gave us the task of making others his friends also. Our message is that God was making all mankind his friends through Christ.' (2 Corinthians 5:17–19a)
Through Jesus Christ's death and resurrection, God has introduced 'a new order'—relationships between God and man, and those between people, can be mended. Christians are given the task of reaching out to others with this life-changing message.

'Be fair in your treatment of one another. Stop taking advantage of aliens, orphans and widows.' (Jeremiah 7:5–6)

'Do not deprive foreigners and orphans of their rights.' (Deuteronomy 24:17)
God's people are to look after the needs of those groups in society whom prejudice and discrimination could harm.

★ ★ ★

'There is no difference between Jews and Gentiles, between slaves and free men, between men and women; you are all one in union with Christ Jesus.' (Galatians 3:28)
There is no place for racial, social or sexual discrimination in God's family—among Christians themselves or in their attitudes to other people.

● **Discrimination** This is a stronger means than prejudice of showing hostility. It is action taken against people in a group we dislike so that they will not have the same opportunities as those who belong to our own group. It goes beyond prejudice because it deprives people of equal status in important areas of daily life.

Black people in the West have often found that, despite legislation, they are discriminated against in the areas of employment, housing and the law; they have to pay higher insurance premiums than most white people do. There is still white prejudice that black people are lazy, dirty and irresponsible.

Discrimination can take two forms. One is open or *overt*, such as when someone is turned down for a job when a less qualified person gets it. The other is *structural*, when the structures in our society operate against someone of another race because they don't know how to complete an application form or what conventions of dress are appropriate at interview.

When people feel that they are being discriminated against, they either give up the struggle to prove themselves equal, forming close communities with their own group (which produces 'ghettos'), or they fight back with a protest. This may take the form of reinforcing their right to their own culture—such as the upsurge of Rastafarianism among West Indian young people—or may involve violence, as seen in inner-city riots.

● **Violence** Discrimination tends to be hidden; it has to be discovered by the person who is being discriminated against. Violence is strong and 'positive'—it is open for all to see. Physical or verbal violence is action taken against an individual or group we dislike in order to keep them weak, fearful or subservient to our own group.

Persecution and expulsion is an even stronger form of violence. Jews were expelled from England under Edward I in 1290, because it was believed (prejudice) that they ritually killed Christian babies. Although it was untrue, it led to an attack upon the Jewish population and a ban on them entering England until the time of Cromwell 400 years later. Thousands of Asians were expelled from Uganda in 1972, because they were considered to be an economic threat to the local population.

● **Extermination** There are a number of tribes which have been totally exterminated by their enemies. When this happens, it is called 'genocide'. The most notorious example of this extreme expression of prejudice was the Nazi attempt to exterminate the Jewish people during the Second World War. Over 6 million Jews were put to death in concentration camps all over Europe in an effort to wipe them out; many more Jews died in this way than currently live in Israel. Genocide is the most violent and extreme form of hostility between one group and another.

Discussion topics

1 'Laws curb behaviour—they can force you to treat me justly, but they can't make you love me.' Can laws and/or education do away with racial (or any other type of) prejudice and discrimination? Have you any other solutions?

2 What evidences are there that class distinction and colour prejudice are still strong today?

3 Has every person the same basic human rights? How would you define them?

4 How far is hostility towards other groups based on: ignorance; stereotyping; fear; feelings of superiority, rather than a knowledge of individuals? How many friends do you have who are white (if you're coloured), coloured (if you're white), handicapped (if you're healthy), healthy (if you're handicapped), or of a different generation?

5 Do you think that the Women's Liberation Movement has helped or hindered the cause of equality for women?

6 Find out and discuss examples (historical and current) of how and why Christians have fought against prejudice and discrimination. Why do you think they get involved in this sort of activity?

UNIT 10

THE MASS MEDIA

It is difficult for us to imagine what it was like centuries ago when there was no printing, no radio or television, no newspapers. News of special events could be spread by bonfires on hill-tops, but the details had to be taken from village to village by messengers or round the streets by town criers. All messages were hand-written, and any important notices were displayed in a public place, such as on a church door.

This sort of situation now seems almost unbelievable, because the twentieth century has seen a communications revolution. Not only can messages be sent very quickly by radio, satellite and cable, but pictures can be transmitted at the same time. The whole world is covered by a communications network—news now travels fast.

A further aspect of this 'revolution' is that the same information can be brought to large numbers of people through the 'mass media': print, film, television, radio, tape, disc and so on.

Uses of the mass media

The mass media can be used for a variety of purposes.

● **To give information** As well as communicating current affairs, information is needed for education, technology, personal development, travel, commerce . . . the reasons are endless. In a world of rapid technical advance, we need access to new knowledge so that it can be put to use, while access to the arts enriches us as human beings. Information previously only available in books can now also be stored on disc, film and tape; computers can retrieve and use the required information quickly. It has been estimated that the total

amount of knowledge in the world doubles every ten years—so efficient storage and speedy retrieval systems are vital to cope with this explosion of knowledge.

● **For entertainment** Cinema, video, radio, television, together with music on disc or cassette, provide for much of our leisure time. Newspapers fulfil a dual role: they provide information—but in a form which the readers enjoy, making them entertaining too.

● **For persuasion** This occurs mostly through advertising in which print, television, radio, mail and other methods are used to persuade people to buy certain products. It is also possible—via the same media—to try to influence people to adopt a particular political or religious viewpoint. When information becomes a powerful means of persuasion, then the media are in danger of being manipulated for propaganda purposes.

Problems and dangers

There are two types of problems associated with the mass media: the **material presented**, and the **effects** of the media.

In the case of the material presented, it is normally a question of truth. In everyday life, when we tell someone a story, it can be completely untrue, or we can miss vital parts out, or we can distort the truth to our own advantage. Exactly the same can happen in the media:

● **Completely untrue** Advertisements have been displayed which say that protein shampoos mend the split ends of hair. Scientists working for consumer protection groups have tested this and found the claim to be completely untrue. If they are right, then a deliberate lie has been used to sell the shampoo.

● **Vital information left out** Politicians in the 1980s correctly said that their party in government had brought down the rate of inflation by 8 per cent, but they failed to say that inflation had risen by more than 8 per cent immediately after they took office. It was not a lie, but a selection of facts which put their performance in the best possible light.

A CHRISTIAN PERSPECTIVE

Christians have always been very interested in communication, because they believe that the good news about new life in Jesus Christ must be communicated to other people. The early Christians held 'mass meetings', such as the gathering on the first Whit Sunday when 3,000 became Christians, but much of their communicating was done person to person, or by travelling from village to village, explaining what Jesus' teaching was all about.

Paul was the most famous of the missionaries, or travelling preachers and teachers, of the early Christian church. His journeys took him throughout modern Turkey and Greece, and eventually to Rome. As well as the spoken word, Paul used written communication: his letters to churches he founded form a large proportion of the New Testament. They were written by hand and copied by church members so that the Christian teaching in them could be more widely circulated.

For centuries, monks copied portions of the Bible by hand and then added beautiful decorations, to produce 'illuminated manuscripts'. For the majority of the population, who could not read or write, stained glass windows were ways of teaching Bible stories to the congregation. Music and drama (the Mystery Plays) were also popular means of conveying Bible truths.

When the communications revolution began with the 'rediscovery' of printing in the fifteenth century, Christians were quick to take advantage of it. The Bible was the first book to go into print, and it is still the world's best-selling title. Christians throughout the world are involved in Bible translation and distribution, so that everyone will have the chance to read the Bible in his own language.

Christians in the twentieth century are involved in the mass media in a variety of ways: for example meetings, radio broadcasting, television, rock concerts, book publishing—all means possible are used to communicate the Christian faith worldwide.

● **Distortion of the truth** A manufacturer of breakfast cereal may correctly say that his product is fortified with vitamins, but he would never reveal that *unless* it was sprayed with vitamins during manufacture, there would be more food value in the packet than in the cereal!

In these situations, the lie or deception is much more serious than my fabrication of a good story to a friend. Through the mass media it is told to many more people; we are more likely to believe it because we somehow expect the media to tell the truth.

The potential for distortion of the facts is enormous. After a television interview, different questions can be spliced in. Or bits can be left out to change the emphasis.

Even the choice of camera angle by a television programme director can completely change the view of an event. For instance, a violent incident may be selected during a demonstration which is mainly completely peaceful.

There is also concern about other possible effects which the mass media may have.

● **Indoctrination** This has several meanings, all concerned with persuading people:

Even photographs can 'lie'. How could this picture be captioned in a newspaper to give two completely different impressions of what was happening?

—to teach something as true when not *everyone* accepts it as true: for example, that the angel Gabriel dictated the *Qur'an* to Muhammad, or that the wafer turns into the flesh of Christ at the Mass;
—to teach something which is not the truth because it is distorted or because the whole truth has not been told: e.g. that the British Empire was entirely benevolent to the peoples in its colonies;
—to make people believe or accept something without giving them chance to think it through properly: e.g. to convince someone that your political views are right just because you treat them well;
—to make people believe something in such a way that they cannot or will not consider any other viewpoint, even though the points against that viewpoint have a lot of weight: e.g. to be unable to consider arguments against monetarism or capital punishment.
The meanings are all subtly different, but they show that indoctrination happens when people are not given *proper* information, i.e.

when the information is not fair or balanced.

● **Corruption of the viewer or reader** When the media continually show bad behaviour, the values can have an effect on people watching or reading. Because the media often present the same things to a large audience, many people are receiving the same message. When the media therefore say or imply that 'everybody is doing this', it is easy to be influenced and say 'OK, I'll do it too', believing that to be the social norm of behaviour, rather than standing out against a crowd.

The media can also influence our ideas of how to treat people. We may have little conception of the horrific

❛ It is now realized that a banquet of sex and violence . . . does not always purge nor satisfy nor eliminate the desire for more, nor . . . does it produce a revolting repugnance. Some evidence suggests that a *desire* may speedily become a *need* which, like drug addiction, escalates a need for more . . . The youths in New York, who after seeing *A Clockwork Orange* went out to perform what they had seen on the screen, support this argument. ❜
From *Images of Man*, by Donald J. Drew

and inhuman ways in which some people behave. But when we are introduced to such actions through the media, it changes our mental make-up—some would say it 'corrupts' us. When people are exposed to bad language on (say) television, violence in films and the press, or unfaithfulness in marriage in plays, they accept this as normal, assume that 'society's like that' and adopt similar standards themselves. Even those who do not become violent or unfaithful themselves often cease to care about the situation or think that it is at all unusual.

● **Corruption of the presenter** Mass media cost money—big money. Wealthy people therefore may be tempted to try to use the media for their own ends. Pop music is an area

where this has aroused concern. If a record is promoted well enough over the radio, sales are assured and the record company is able to make a substantial profit. Disc jockeys could be put under pressure by powerful

❛ It may be rightly asked whether, in spite of all his conquests, man is not turning back against himself the results of his activity; having rationally controlled nature, man is now becoming a slave of the things he makes. ❜
Pope Paul VI

business interests to accept bribes to promote their latest records.

● **Invasion of privacy** Viewers, listeners and readers like to know personal details about other people's lives—particularly the rich, famous or infamous. *This is Your Life* is one of the longest-running television programmes in the UK; chat-shows draw large audiences; biographies are one of the most popular types of literature. There is therefore a continual temptation for those in the media to 'use' people. Reporters not only sit in the courts so that they can tell the world the (often unsavoury) details about a case, but information is obtained from informants, telephone calls, snap interviews and any other means available. To do this involves exploiting people for their news or entertainment value—often their griefs, worries, problems or sorrows are made public through the media.

● **Suggestion** Suggestion is a special form of indoctrination and corruption of the receiver: it is used to communicate to people at a subconscious level so that they are not aware that it is happening. In adverts, for example, no dishonest claims are made for the product, but the setting conveys a certain impression: a handsome man appears after a girl has used a particular shampoo or perfume; alcoholic drinks are always served in a pleasant, sociable environment. An appeal is made to our basic instincts —in these cases, to our sex instinct and our social instinct. The

We are used to receiving 'instant' news of world-wide events via the mass media. But can we always rely on their unbiassed reporting?

WHAT THE BIBLE SAYS

'Do not desire another man's house; do not desire his wife . . . or anything else that he owns.' (Exodus 20:17)

'I have learnt to be satisfied with what I have.' (Philippians 4:11)
Contentment, not covetousness, should characterize the Christian. Advertising has to be looked at critically in this light.

★ ★ ★

'Do not steal or cheat or lie.' (Leviticus 19:11)
Information should be true, balanced, honestly come by and not involve anyone in 'corrupt' dealings.

★ ★ ★

'Jesus said to his disciples, ''Things that make people fall into sin are bound to happen, but how terrible for the one who makes them happen! It would be better for him if a large millstone were tied round his neck and he were thrown into the sea than for him to cause one of these little ones to sin.''' (Luke 17:1–2)
The young, innocent and vulnerable should be protected, not exploited.

advertiser is aiming directly at the emotions, not the mind.

Assignments and discussion topics

1 In what ways have the mass media given us the feeling of living in a 'global village'? What are the advantages and disadvantages of this?

2 Try to find and discuss examples of advertisements which illustrate: exploitation; appeal to materialistic values; propaganda; distortion of the facts; suggestion; waste.

3 'An audience has the right to choose to see perversion if it wants to. Censorship is undemocratic.' Do you agree? Or do you think there should be some censorship of books, films, plays, videos, cable television?

4 Do the mass media stop us thinking for ourselves?

5 Do you impose any restrictions on yourself in terms of what you choose to watch/read/hear? How do you decide? Do you think the Christian standards mentioned in this unit are important for the general well-being of society? For instance, ought society to be protected from pornography as it is from disease?

UNIT 11

CRIME

You can break a moral law by cheating, or a religious law by refusing to pray five times a day (if you are a Muslim). You can break a social custom by exercising your dog at three o'clock in the morning. None of these is a *crime* unless the state has made a law which either forbids or insists on it.

A crime is committed when a law made by the state is broken. Criminal law is always made by the state (parliament) and the courts, and is very precisely defined. It applies to everyone, and the state decrees the punishment if the law is broken.

Despite their limitations, crime statistics do seem to show an overall increase in the number of offences committed, which many people see as a worrying trend.

? Why do you think crime is on the increase in our society?

? Which of the statistics shown cause you the most concern?

Causes

When the police are hunting a criminal, they obviously look for clues. But they also try to discover whether the suspect had the **opportunity** and a **motive** for committing the crime.

There are many motives for crime: desperation, thrill, boredom, frustration, anger, jealousy, greed . . . and many more. However, a motive is usually regarded as an 'immediate cause'—the event or feeling which finally brought about the crime. For every crime, there are also deeper, underlying, 'intermediate causes'. An analysis of the percentage figures in the table overleaf giving a break-down of particular crimes by age-group and sex might suggest both immediate and intermediate causes.

? What general differences can you

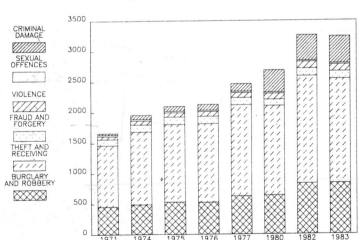

CRIMINAL OFFENCES
in England and Wales (thousands)

CRIMINAL DAMAGE
SEXUAL OFFENCES
VIOLENCE
FRAUD AND FORGERY
THEFT AND RECEIVING
BURGLARY AND ROBBERY

BUT:
1983 figures for sex offences include offences of gross indecency with a child for the first time.
1982 and 83 figures for theft and receiving include stealing of electricity for the first time.
1982 and 83 figures for criminal damage include amounts of damage less than £20: this was not included in 1971.
This illustrates some of the problems in comparing statistics!

Percentages of age-groups of men and women responsible for particular crimes in England and Wales, 1983

Age group	10/13		14/16		17/20		21+	
Sex	M	F	M	F	M	F	M	F
murder/manslaughter	0	0	5	0	17	0	78	0
violence	3	6	15	29	29	22	52	43
sexual offences	5	11	17	15	19	20	59	54
burglary	11	17	27	29	30	27	32	27
robbery	6	9	16	29	33	34	45	28
theft/handling	12	16	23	21	23	15	42	48
fraud/forgery	1	1	5	6	19	25	75	68
criminal damage	15	11	20	23	29	19	36	46
others (not motoring)	0	0	3	3	22	24	75	73
motoring	0	0	6	4	24	15	70	81

NB The figures represent the percentage of a particular crime committed by a particular sex in a particular age group.

detect between crimes committed by men/women, older women/younger women, older men/younger men?
? Can you think of reasons (physical/psychological/social) which might help to explain the statistics?

There are important psychological explanations for crime. Freud, the eminent Jewish psychologist from Vienna, believed that we are all born with basically selfish instincts and desires. If those instincts remained uncontrolled, we would all be criminals. However, most of us learn —by being told, and from experience—that it is not acceptable to go ahead and satisfy all our desires and instincts without regard for anyone else. Some people never learn this, either from other people or from experience: it is these people who become criminals.

Psychologists also say that the kind of behaviour which society wants from us has to be learned. Some people find it hard to learn what is expected, just as others find it hard to learn foreign languages or science, and they then become criminals.

There are also social theories of crime. Experiments have shown that if laboratory rats are put into a cage, they will live quite happily together so long as there are not too many of them. If there *are* too many, and if there is a lot of noise in the lab, the rats become violent and attack each other. Similarly, it is thought that when human beings live in overcrowded conditions under pressure, they react in the same kind of way.

One of the strongest pressures in modern society is materialism. Everything encourages us to want a large house, a new car, the latest gadgets, new clothes and foreign holidays. *But* these are not available to everyone. Those who cannot obtain the material possessions they want in such a society may become so frustrated that they use unacceptable (criminal) ways of getting them. This could explain why so much crime consists of burglary, robbery and criminal damage. In England and Wales in 1983, 18 per cent of crimes of violence, 38 per cent of burglaries, 35 per cent of crimes of theft and 35 per cent of criminal damage committed by men, was committed by young people below the age of sixteen. (See the table.)

The heart of the matter?

There is probably *some* truth in *all* these ideas, but certain facts confound the theories. Many children from 'poor' homes where everything is against them do not commit any crime. Conversely, there are people with all possible advantages who turn out to be vicious and dangerous criminals. How do we explain that?

Many Christians believe that beneath all the motives and the

Vandalism is often a protest by young people against a society which makes them feel failures. They attack things that are part of 'the system'—schools, buses, trains, bus shelters, official buildings. Vandalism is not 'mindless' or 'pointless' to those who commit it.

intermediate causes, everyone has a nature which is basically evil. Jesus said that it was not external things which are the root cause of our problem, but the feelings, attitudes and desires which are internal and which lead to evil actions. This natural tendency to do wrong is sometimes called 'original sin'.

Christians believe that it is as this evil nature reacts with or against the social situation or the learning difficulty that the origin and explanation of crime is to be found. If you are sceptical about this, just ask yourself why it is that something inside you automatically seems to rebel against rules and laws. When we know the course of action we *should* take, we seem to have an inbuilt bias to want to do the exact opposite!

Crime and punishment

What should be done when a person has committed a crime? Most people agree that the offender should be punished in some way or other. But what form should the punishment take? What are we trying to do when we punish someone?

In the Western world, there are a number of 'theories of punishment':
● **The theory of retribution** This is the idea that if a person has done something wrong, he should be made

to pay for it. His punishment is considered fair because he is 'getting what he deserves'. This approach concentrates on the crime itself, and runs the risk of completely overlooking the personal circumstances of the criminal. But it satisfies strict justice and (some would argue) the criminal's own need for the crime to be fully paid off.
● **The theory of protection** If someone sets out to disrupt society and commits criminal acts, he should be removed from the community so that other people are protected from

METHODS OF PUNISHMENT
Read through the list below. Try to find out:
? Which methods of punishment can be used by a court?
? Which methods of punishment are used for which offences?
? Which punishments fit which theories?
Attendance Centre Juveniles and young adult offenders can be made to go to an attendance centre for 12 or 24 hours in 2-hour sessions, normally on a Saturday afternoon.
Binding over The offender pays money into court as a pledge that he will return to court if required and that he will behave himself. If he fails to keep his pledge, he loses his money.
Capital punishment (death penalty) The offender's life is taken away by firing squad, hanging, electrocution, etc.
Community Service Order The offender is required to work (unpaid) for between 40 and 240 hours within a 12-month period to help others in the community.
Compensation The offender may be made to pay compensation to his victim(s), as well as being punished in other ways.
Corporal punishment Injury to the human body, normally by lashing or caning. In extreme cases under Islamic law, a thief's hand may be cut off.
Criminal bankruptcy An offender whose crime causes a large financial loss can be made to face bankruptcy

There is growing concern over the dangerously overcrowded conditions in many prisons. Also, the system may punish but it does not seem to reform—many ex-convicts turn back to crime when their sentence is over and land themselves in prison again.

proceedings, as well as being punished in other ways.
Day Training Centre Attendance is required for up to 60 days so that the offender can receive education or vocational training which may help him to get a job.
Deferrment of sentence Sentence can be deferred for up to 6 months so that the court can take into account the person's behaviour between their first appearance and the passing of sentence.
Deprivation of property Any property used in a crime can be taken away.
Detoxification centre Habitual drunken offenders can be taken to such a centre to be 'dried out' and to receive social and medical help.
Discharge No punishment is considered appropriate under the

circumstances. The discharge can be 'absolute', with no strings attached, or 'conditional'—no more offences within a specified period, of up to 3 years.
Disqualification Loss of a driving licence.
Fine The payment of money into court.
Imprisonment Imprisonment can be imposed for any term up to 'life', the severity of the sentence depending on the supposed danger to the community of the offender. In the UK, there is so much pressure on the prison system that a Committee of Inquiry has recommended that many people at present punished by imprisonment (for example, habitual drunkards, the mentally ill or inadequate, defaulters on fines) should be punished in other, more appropriate ways.
Probation Order The offender is set free, but has to keep certain conditions laid down by the court, must make sure that he keeps out of trouble, and must keep in touch with a probation officer, who will try to help him through (and sometimes beyond) his period on probation.

WHAT THE BIBLE SAYS

'"Worship no god but me . . .
"Do not bow down to any idol or worship it . . .
"Do not use my name for evil purposes . . .
"Observe the Sabbath and keep it holy . . .
"Respect your father and your mother . . .
"Do not commit murder.
"Do not commit adultery.
"Do not steal.
"Do not accuse anyone falsely.
"Do not desire another man's house . . . or anything else that he owns."'
(Exodus 20:3–17)

The Ten Commandments were given originally to the Israelites, and have formed the basis for the moral law in many countries throughout the world. Responsibilities to God and to other people are combined in God's laws.

★   ★   ★

'I know that good does not live in me—that is, in my human nature. For even though the desire to do good is in me, I am not able to do it. I don't do the good I want to do; instead, I do the evil that I do not want to do.' (Romans 7:18–19)

A realistic view of human nature is that its inbuilt tendency is towards evil actions, not good. It is not just a person's social conditions that predispose him towards crime. Creeds or ideologies which do not allow for this, e.g. communism, are not being realistic or true to the way things are.

★   ★   ★

'Everyone must obey the state authorities, because no authority exists without God's permission, and the existing authorities have been put there by God. Whoever opposes the existing authority opposes what God has ordered; and anyone who does so will bring judgement on himself . . . you must obey the authorities—not just because of God's punishment, but also as a matter of conscience.' (Romans 13:1–2, 5)

An authority structure is God-ordered and God-given (although power and authority can be misused or abused), and to disobey or resist civil rulers is to disobey or resist God.

★   ★   ★

'Anyone who commits murder shall be put to death, and anyone who kills an animal belonging to someone else must replace it. The principle is a life for a life.' (Leviticus 24:17–18)

The Old Testament law had elements of retribution, deterrence and compensation when a crime was committed.

★   ★   ★

'The teachers of the Law and the Pharisees brought in a woman who had been caught committing adultery . . . "Teacher," they said to Jesus, "this woman was caught in the very act of committing adultery. In our Law Moses commanded that such a woman must be stoned to death. Now, what do you say?" . . .
'Jesus . . . said to them, "Whichever one of you has committed no sin may throw the first stone at her." . . . When they heard this, they all left, one by one, the older ones first. Jesus was left alone, with the woman still standing there. He . . . said to her, "Where are they? Is there no one left to condemn you?"
'"No one, sir," she answered.
'"Well, then," Jesus said, "I do not condemn you either. Go, but do not sin again."' (John 8:3–11)

Jesus himself clearly believed that the law must be tempered by mercy. We have all sinned.

★   ★   ★

'Never take revenge . . . For the scripture says, "I will take revenge, I will pay back, says the Lord." Instead . . . "If your enemy is hungry, feed him; if he is thirsty, give him a drink . . ." Do not let evil defeat you; instead, conquer evil with good.' (Romans 12:19–21)

Christians are not to take revenge on someone who has wronged them, but rather to show love, kindness and forgiveness.

★   ★   ★

'For sin pays its wage—death; but God's free gift is eternal life in union with Christ our Lord.' (Romans 6:23)

Death, or separation from God, is the automatic consequence of sin. Nothing sinful can exist in the perfect light of God's presence.

★   ★   ★

'Everyone must die once, and after that be judged by God.' (Hebrews 9:27)

There is a 'day of reckoning' for everyone after death—even for those who seem to have 'got away with it' during their lifetime.

★   ★   ★

'Christ himself carried our sins in his body to the cross, so that we might die to sin and live for righteousness. It is by his wounds that you have been healed.' (1 Peter 2:24)

Christians believe that when Jesus died, he took the death penalty due to them. Because God is just, he cannot 'turn a blind eye' to evil, but because he is loving, he has provided a way of forgiveness. Jesus died so that a free pardon is available to anyone who asks.

---

his anti-social behaviour. A murderer is imprisoned for life so that he cannot kill again; a thief is imprisoned so that people's belongings will be safe.

● **The theory of deterrence** If a criminal is severely punished, he will not do the same thing again, and his punishment will put others off as well. However, in many cases, this theory manifestly does not work. Just as there are names which appear in the school punishment book over and over again, so there are 'hardened' criminals who continue to commit crimes. They are obviously not deterred by the thought of punishment.

There is also concern at an element of injustice in this approach: if the punishment should 'fit the crime', it is hardly right that a person should receive a punishment out of all proportion to what he has done simply to deter others.

● **The theory of reform** Punishment should be seen as 'treatment', because crime is a disease to be healed, not a fault to be punished. To some people, this does

The Caliph's problem

A Persian ruler, the Caliph, wished to increase his power over his subjects, and to make his influence more widely felt. His advisers suggested that he should increase the number of laws and declare that the punishment for breaking any one of them would be thirty lashes.

When he met his advisers at their next meeting, he told them that he needed more advice. His aged mother had broken the new laws. If he had her beaten, it would kill her and would prove to everyone that he had no love. If he let her off, it would bring his kingdom to an end because he would be seen to be unjust.

The advisers were stumped: they could not see how his love and his justice could both be satisfied.

But the Caliph found a way.

He ordered that his mother be brought before the court. She was found guilty of breaking the new laws and sentenced to thirty lashes. Then, having passed sentence, the Caliph descended the steps from his throne and went to where his mother was standing. He took her by the arm, and gently led her up the steps and seated her on his throne. Then he took off his own robe, descended the steps again into the courtroom and received the thirty lashes on his own back.

The Caliph was shown to be a man who was full of love, but perfectly just.

---

not appear to be punishment at all—it might be very gracious to forgive all criminals and give them another chance, but is it just?

> ❝ Whenever you find a man who says he does not believe in a real Right and Wrong, you will find the same man going back on this a moment later. He may break his promise to you, but if you try breaking one to him he will be complaining "It's not fair" . . . Human beings, all over the earth, have this curious idea that they ought to behave in a certain way, and cannot really get rid of it . . . (But) they do not in fact behave in that way . . . These two facts are the foundation of all clear thinking about ourselves and the universe we live in. ❞
> C. S. Lewis

● The theory of vindication

Crime must be punished so that the law is not brought into disrepute. If a rule of any kind is made, and people break it, they need to be punished so that the law will command respect and the rule of law can be maintained.

Such an approach is taken by many Christians, together with a willingness to try to help and reform. Christians believe that punishment and forgiveness *can* go together: punishment must be given for the wrongdoing so that the law or rules can be upheld, but they would still forgive the *person* who has done wrong.

Discussion topics

1 What would you say to the statement that the only 'commandment' worth bothering about is 'Thou shalt not get caught'?

2 Do you think that imprisonment does more harm than good?

3 People who supported the abolition of the death penalty did so because they felt that it cannot deter or reform the offender, it does not deter others, justice is sometimes miscarried and the act of taking someone's life makes society yet more violent. What do you think?

HOUSING

What is the difference between a house and a home? We talk about 'moving house'—we clean it up, move furniture in, get things straight and tidy. Once all this has been done, we usually use the word 'home' and invite people to come round.

But a house or housing unit is not necessarily a *home*. When people refer to a 'good home', they do not mean that the bricks and mortar are of good quality or that the woodwork is sound. A house becomes a home when people feel that they belong there. For many people, the feeling of belonging comes from being a member of a family where there is love, care and security.

For people who live alone, the feeling of being 'at home', of belonging, comes from the way that they have put their 'belongings' together: the furniture, decorations and personal effects reflect the feelings, likes and dislikes of the person who lives there, so that they feel secure and happy when they are among them.

You may live in a beautiful stately 'home' and yet experience less love and affection than in a close-knit family in a cramped little terrace. However, some people's actual *houses* are in such poor condition that love gets frayed at the edges and there is little security to be enjoyed. For them, bad housing is not a 'national scandal' (as politicians are fond of saying) but a desperate personal situation, making a real 'home' a virtual impossibility.

The cost of housing

A house is the most costly thing you are ever likely to buy. The price paid is usually about four times your total annual salary. As a house-owner, you then have to pay rates; on leasehold property, you sometimes pay 'ground

BUYING A HOUSE

DEPOSIT / LEGAL FEES / MORTGAGE

Institutions which lend money to prospective house-buyers have to satisfy themselves that their loan will be repaid. They are unlikely to consider unemployed or poorly-paid people or single parents, for example, as 'a good risk'. People in such circumstances may also find it hard to raise enough money for a deposit. Home-ownership therefore tends to widen the gap between the 'haves' and the 'have-nots' in society.

rent' to the owner of the land on which the property is built. You have to pay for repairs and make sure that the house and garden are maintained properly. It is a very costly business!

However, people who buy houses do get benefits which others do not have: local authority improvement grants, certain tax concessions and a possession which increases in value.

If you cannot buy a house, the alternative is to pay rent weekly or monthly to the person who owns the house where you live. Some houses are owned by private landlords, but the majority (council housing) is now owned by local authorities.

Private landlords are often not prepared to spend much money on improving their property. It is difficult for them to get their money back by raising the rent, because the law protects tenants from large rent increases. Many landlords have therefore sold their houses to avoid this kind of problem, and this has had several results:

● There is far less rented accommodation available—people wanting to rent a house or flat often cannot find one.
● People in good rented accommodation may be paying almost as much per month as someone who is buying their own house, but will have nothing to show for it.
● People paying a reasonable rent often live in poor quality housing.

The problem of poor housing

A survey undertaken in England in 1981 found that 1,120,000 houses (6.2 per cent) were unfit to live in, because they were dangerous to health and well-being; 910,000 houses (5 per cent) were substandard because they lacked one of the basic necessities such as a bath, inside toilet or a place to cook food. Taken together, these figures represented 10 per cent of all housing units in England.

Other surveys have shown that the rate of repair and improvement of houses is exactly the same as that of decay from 'satisfactory' to 'unsatisfactory' houses, where disrepair has led to dampness and rot. This is not only a huge personal problem for the occupants, but also a social problem: poor housing is almost always associated with poor health, low educational standards, overcrowding, the breakdown of family life, violence and crime.

Letter of despair
The problem with looking at the statistics of acute deprivation is that it is easy to forget that each statistic is an individual person. This letter from a mother in Liverpool to *The Daily Mirror* was published in the aftermath of the Toxteth riots, and brings the housing problem onto a disturbingly personal level:

❜ I am writing my story hopeful that you will consider printing it. The motive being that someone in authority with council housing will read it and realize what they can do to decent people.

'My family consists of my husband and two children. We are like most couples of today who find it a struggle to keep the family united in difficult conditions. We are living with in-laws which is a problem in itself. We had applied to be put on to the Liverpool housing list. It seemed as if we were on it for an eternity, when at last we were sent an offer of accommodation. They offered us the choice of one of the worst areas in Liverpool. In fact, they offered us two other areas which were just as bad. Choosing the best of a bad lot was difficult. So we tossed a coin to decide our future home.

INSIDE LOCAL GOVERNMENT

Your local authority offices will be located at your civic centre, town hall or municipal buildings. There are many departments involved in aspects of housing whose main responsibilities are outlined below:
● **The Planning Department** has to make sure that new houses or extensions to existing houses are built so that they fit into an area and are not an eyesore, and that services such as shops, schools and open spaces are provided.
● **The Engineering Department** has to make sure that houses are built according to certain building regulations, so that they are safe and will survive bad weather. Often the department will administer grants which enable house-owners to repair or modernize their property.
● **The Environmental Health Department** has to make sure that houses are maintained properly and are fit to live in. It can compel owners to make repairs, order the demolition of houses, and use the law to prevent overcrowding.
● **The Housing Department** can provide houses for rent, and, having done so, has to maintain them properly. It has to find accommodation for homeless people in its area.

'Our marriage was under a great strain, so we accepted the offer. It was a bottom-floor maisonette in a disgusting state. I sat on the stairs of this dump and felt like being sick. It was absolutely filthy. I was six months' pregnant and really desperate for our own place. But I never dreamed we would have to go so low as to accept an offer like this. But with one child and another on the way (plus living with in-laws) there was no way out but to say yes to the offer. It took us three months to get it into a liveable condition. In fact, the night before I had my baby we had just finished decorating the hall.

'My husband works in a factory which is doubtful of its future. He is on short time, so we can't go in for buying our own home, because his wages are so low. So we are stuck on this estate. We cannot move out because the would-be big noises say a bottom-floor maisonette is classed as a house and will not move us out.

'We are quiet people who keep ourselves to ourselves. We don't cause anybody any bother. My eldest child hates playing outside because there is always fighting. He is a good child who is slowly being moulded into an animal. I watch it helplessly every day. I can't keep him in—he needs to be out playing. He has started spitting out for no reason. His manners are going, and he used to be so polite.

'He talks of his friends robbing houses (it is free talk around here about how many houses they rob). He wanted me to have a game of cops and robbers. But it was not the game it used to be. He played the robber, but it was more cops and muggers. He pretended to steal my bag off my arm. I was absolutely horrified.

'My child is only six years old. When I try to teach him not to be like them the reply I get is heartbreaking. He says if he does not do what the other kids say they will gang up on him and he gets scared when they all start

hitting him. How can anyone possibly win in this situation?

'If I leave my baby in his pram outside the front door the people upstairs start washing the landing without a care for who is underneath. The baby gets soaked. It's worth seeing to believe. We get stones and cans thrown at the door. I am too scared to leave the baby outside any more because he may get hit by stones or any objects thrown his way.

'I feel like I am on the verge of a nervous breakdown. Our marriage is still in jeopardy. I would like to ask any council official how they would react to seeing their children or grandchildren being subjected to these conditions.

'My child is slowly going off the rails, so to speak, and it's because the council officials think we should be grateful for anything they offer, knowing fully they have the upper hand when people like us are desperate for a home. We are slowly being destroyed as a decent family. There must be a way out of places like this but what price do we pay? What price would council officials pay if it were their children?

'I hope you print this letter. I can't get to the depth of the matter. It would take a month of Sundays. But I hope it will make some of them sit up and take notice.'

There are two ways in which poor housing can be improved. First, a 'slum clearance programme' can be undertaken by the local authority. The old buildings are completely demolished and new homes are built, either in the same place or on a new estate outside the area. In times of recession the amount of new housing built is not normally as great as the number of homes which become slums, so that there is a general deterioration. Local authority funds are limited, so replacement housing on the same spot has tended in the past to be high-rise flats.

This approach has proved to have several social consequences:
● New out-of-town estates often mean higher rents combined with higher cost of transport to work, which some cannot afford.

ACTION FOR THE HOMELESS

The film *Cathy Come Home*, shown on BBC television in 1966, stirred consciences about the plight of homeless people. As a result of the gifts of money sent to the Christian press, the organization known as **Shelter**, the National Campaign for the Homeless, was set up.

Five national housing charities joined forces to raise money for housing associations and to make the problem of homelessness more widely known. In the first year over £2 million was raised.

Shelter became involved in other projects too. It has tried to work within communities to encourage them to help themselves. It has established Housing Aid Centres in a number of cities where people with housing problems can go for free help and advice. It uses the knowledge gained through the centres to put pressure on local and central government to improve the situation.

The **National Cyrenians** are another organization concerned with the homeless. They link together groups who have set up small houses to provide accommodation for single, homeless people. Some centres provide night shelters; others provide long-stay accommodation to give more extended help to those who need it.

People are accepted into Cyrenian centres no matter what state they are in, but they are not allowed to take alcohol or other drugs within the centre. None of the centres is large: they normally each take between eight and fifteen people, and the workers are volunteers.

When people are accepted into a Cyrenian centre, they become members of the community, which makes its own rules and arrangements. There is a weekly house meeting where decisions are taken. In this way, those who are not used to taking decisions or working with others learn how to cope with situations they will meet when they return to normal society.

WHAT THE BIBLE SAYS

Among the many who are concerned about poverty and homelessness are Christians, who have an additional motivation — they know from the Bible what God feels about the situation.

'You shall set the fiftieth year apart and proclaim freedom to all the inhabitants of the land. During this year all property that has been sold shall be restored to the original owner or his descendants . . .' (Leviticus 25:10)

If a man had to sell his house to pay off a debt, it had to be returned to him (or his family) in the 'Year of Jubilee', which occurred once in every fifty years. This was to avoid concentration of land in the hands of a few wealthy landowners, and their exploitation of debtors.

★   ★   ★

'The Lord says . . . "The kind of fasting I want is this: Remove the chains of oppression and the yoke of injustice, and let the oppressed go free. Share your food with the hungry and open your homes to the homeless poor. Give clothes to those who have nothing to wear, and do not refuse to help your own relatives."' (Isaiah 58:6–7)

At a time when the Jewish people were keen on religious ritual, God said through his prophet that what he wanted to see was concern for the poor, weak and oppressed.

★   ★   ★

'Jesus said, "Whenever you did this [gave food to the hungry, drink to the thirsty, gave hospitality to a stranger, clothes to the needy, visited the sick or prisoners] for one of the least important of these brothers of mine, you did it for me!"' (Matthew 25:40)

Jesus said that providing for people in need is an important way for Christians to show that they are following and serving him — and it's like doing the same thing for Jesus himself.

★   ★   ★

'Suppose there are brothers or sisters who need clothes and don't have enough to eat. What good is there in your saying to them, "God bless you! Keep warm and eat well!" — if you don't give them the necessities of life?' (James 2:15–16)

'Actions speak louder than words' — helping the poor is a demonstration of faith in action, an outworking of what Christians believe about the love of God.

● New surroundings are unfamiliar, leading to feelings of isolation and loneliness, particularly among old people.
● Well-established and close-knit communities are torn apart.
● High-rise flats have been found to be dangerous and difficult places to live in, especially for old people, and families with young children.

The second approach to the improvement of old houses is through housing associations. These are charities formed to purchase and

> ❛ Everyone has the right to a standard of living adequate for the health and security of their family, including . . . a home. ❜
> *United Nations Declaration of Human Rights*

rebuild old property, so that it can then be let at a reasonable rent. Government grants can be obtained towards this work. Some churches have formed housing associations so that they can build property for rent on church-owned land. For example, the Quakers have actively encouraged their members to become involved, particularly where housing associations have been set up to meet the needs of special groups, such as the elderly or disabled. In such cases, 'sheltered housing' is often provided: single-storey dwellings are linked together with a warden's flat and community facilities.

Individual house-owners can, of course, renovate and improve their own property, but the schemes just outlined are concerned with people who cannot afford their own homes. In 1982, 78,000 households had to be provided with accommodation by local authorities because they had priority needs such as pregnancy or the presence of dependent children. By 1983, this had risen to 83,000. These people had nowhere to live. The figures do not include people without priority needs. The English and Welsh house condition survey

For some people, 'squatting' in empty property (which is illegal) is a desperate bid to obtain some kind of shelter. For others, it is a social protest. Conditions endured by squatters are often appalling.

showed that in 1981 1,200,000 dwellings out of 19,100,000 were unfit for habitation.

Poor housing is one of the key factors in our society separating the poor from the relatively wealthy. It is the people who are poor who:
● cannot buy houses of their own, so do not get the benefits of grants, tax relief and a possession that increases in value;
● find it difficult and daunting to make contact with local authority officials to get the help they need;
● are condemned to living in slum property or have to sleep rough;
● despair of their situation and find themselves caught in the 'poverty trap'.

Discussion topics

1 Do you agree with the UN Declaration of Human Rights about housing? Why do you think they consider a home to be so important?

2 Should relatively few people be able to buy luxuries when so many haven't even basic necessities?

3 What are some of the problems of 'high-rise living'?

UNIT 13

AUTHORITY

Everywhere we turn there are rules, rules, rules. If you go out with friends for an evening, you may have to be home by a certain time. One of your friends had to 'stay in' after school because she had been late three times in one week. You play snooker, and check the rule about having a foot on the floor when making a shot. When parking the car, you avoid double yellow lines . . .

Why should we keep all these rules? Obviously, if there were no rules and everybody did what they liked, the result would be chaos. If there is no social agreement about whether to drive on the left or right side of the road, the result would be . . . dangerous! Anarchy, do what you like, no rules at all . . . nobody really believes in that.

There are basically two main ways of drawing up the rules. The first is for the biggest or strongest or wealthiest to say 'Do what *I* tell you. From now on I'll make up the rules.' This is the way of totalitarian regimes. And we may be told not only which side of the road to drive on, but also what we are to believe and how we are to behave.

The other way is for society to select people to make up the rules for all the different areas of life. At best, this is the way of democracy. We choose people to represent us, to govern us, to decide how things should be run.

Authorities and authority

We also give to the chosen representatives of the people the authority to maintain order in society. The police, for instance, are 'the arm of the law'—enforcing laws made by leaders appointed by us, the people. We may not *like* the laws.

We may prefer to steal sweets than to pay for them. But so long as there is social agreement that the community works best when people don't just take what doesn't belong to them, the police will continue to stop us stealing. So:
● The authorities, such as police and magistrates, have been given certain powers in society.
● They have been given them by government, i.e. people we have elected to run the country.
● Laws must normally have broad social agreement to work, even though not everyone agrees with all of them.

For instance, football needs certain rules if it is not going to be just a free-for-all. It is agreed that it makes for a better game if there is agreement on how it is to be played, what things are not allowed and so on. Society—or rather, all the football clubs and teams—gives to the Football Association the authority to draw up the rules. The FA then gives to the referee the authority to

A football referee is given authority by the game's governing body to keep the rules of the game. Imagine what would happen if players could do anything they liked without rules at all . . .

apply them in a particular match. The game only works if people play by the rules, don't cheat, don't punch the ref . . . in other words, if authority is respected and obeyed. So:

● When a club leader tells you what you are or are not allowed to do, he has been given authority by the club's management committee *on behalf of the club*.

● When a bill comes to say that the rates are due, it comes from the local council who have been given authority to charge rates *on behalf of the local community*.

● When a magistrate docks you three points for speeding, he is doing so with the authority of the courts and the legal system *on behalf of society*.

The basis for law

So laws, or the rules of the game, are based on authority given by society to its rulers. But where do the basic laws come from?

What is acceptable to society is based on broad agreement on moral issues. These usually go back for centuries, into the traditional values and norms of a particular society. They may be based originally on what has been found to work best: this 'pragmatic' view often underlies

decisions taken by governments today. For instance, the community works best if people do not steal other people's wives, or property, or land, or food.

In the West, Christian views have formed the basis for many of the 'moral' points agreed by society. The Ten Commandments of the Jewish-Christian law lay down basic moral attitudes. Christians also claim that conforming to these laws is the way that society works best—because it was designed that way, by God.

In Eastern countries, other religious traditions have formed different values and social norms. The caste system in India, for instance, is based on Hinduism. Pakistan is changing the laws inherited from the West to fit in with its new aim of being an Islamic state. Other Islamic states, such as Iran, enforce laws that would be unacceptable in Britain, for instance.

Protests

In today's world, many people do not accept the authority of their government. They express this by protest, demonstration, sometimes riots. There are various reasons for this:

● **Totalitarian regimes** When governments have not been elected,

people protest or work for the overthrow of a bad government, because they have no democratic voice at elections.

● **Power of the state** When the state becomes something separate from the people who have elected it, it loses social acceptance, and runs the danger of doing things for reasons other than the good of the people. In his book, *Nineteen Eighty-four*, George Orwell showed the consequences of a state which became something separate from the people—doing away with people who would not toe the line, for instance.

● **Bad government** When laws are passed which are bad or unacceptable, people protest. In a democracy, the way to do so is to get the law changed—for instance, by pressure-groups—as well, of course, as by the normal processes of election of representatives to government. But when people lose patience with democratic processes, they take to the streets to try to force the hand of the government. The danger, of course, is that democracy becomes mob rule. When people take part in protests and demonstrations, bypassing their elected representatives, are they undermining democracy itself?

● **Change the system!** Marxist groups believe that there must be opposition using force to a regime —revolution—if a system is to be changed. So Marxists use marches or protest demonstrations to forward the cause of revolution—even if the aim of the protest or march is quite different.

● **Civil disobedience** On some moral issues, people believe that the cause is so important that opposition to the government is necessary— nuclear weapons, for instance, or abortion laws, or freedom of religion. If it comes to the choice, 'We must obey God rather than men', as Peter said of the early Christian church.

Changing the system

Revolution and protest are ways of trying to change the government or social system by force. One of the reasons protest marches and demonstrations have proved so successful in appealing to public opinion is because of the influence of

A CHRISTIAN PERSPECTIVE

Responsibility
The Old Testament teaches that good government, like the family, is part of the structure of society. The New Testament also shows that the Christian should respect civil authorities, pay taxes ('Render unto Caesar the things that are Caesar's,' Jesus said), pray for governments and leaders.

In the Bible there is also the strong tradition of social protest. The Old Testament prophets protested against rulers who were unjust and corrupt or who took advantage of the poor. In the New Testament, Christians were taught to respect the state, but only as far as the state's powers should go—not when it went against the commands of God. And those were the days of a corrupt and decadent

Roman Empire. If it came to the crunch, the Christians were to obey God rather than men.

They were, however, to work within society to change it, not overthrow it. Jesus was constantly expected to lead a revolution against the occupying Romans. But again and again he showed that his way was to change society from within. Christians are to be like 'lights in a dark world'. They should love, not hate.

Jesus himself went to crucifixion on a trumped-up charge rather than use violence or try to overthrow the opposition of the authorities. The amazing thing was that he achieved more through his death than he would have done if he had seemed to 'win', by escaping from his accusers. His death for human sinfulness was the real victory.

Anti-nuclear demonstrators take to the streets in an attempt to show their strength of feeling about government policies. Is it right to try to force governments to change policies by protests and rallies? Or should people try to get change by democratic processes?

proposals for change or reform. Because the member of parliament has been elected by a particular constituency, he or she is 'representative' of the people—as an individual or a member of a political party.

Another way of 'changing the system' is to get together with others so that the voice is that of many rather than one. The Trades Union movement, for instance, started with a group of Methodist lay preachers. Its concern has been to represent workers who would be exploited by industry and commerce if they did not stand up for their rights.

television. Television news is always looking for something visual to report. A march with banners makes better television than a speaker in parliament! So, many pressure-groups and activists see this as the major means of appealing to public opinion.

But in a parliamentary democracy public opinion must ultimately persuade *parliament* if there is to be a change in the laws. Anyone can stand for election, both to a local council and to parliament. If elected, he or she can put views, questions,

Assignments and discussion topics

1 List all the laws, rules and regulations that affect you in everyday life (home, school, work, travel . . .) and try to categorize them according to whether they are:
   (a) criminal laws (i.e. you can be prosecuted for disobeying them);
   (b) social duties and obligations;
   (c) family habits and conventions;
   (d) useful instructions or guidelines.
In each case, state the reason (or lack of it, if you feel there isn't one) behind the rule.

2 Over the period of a week, list all the examples you can find from radio, television, newspapers and magazines of people rejecting authority (at any level). In each case, say whether:
   (a) they are protesting against bad government, bad laws or bad enforcement;
   (b) you think they are justified or not, giving your reasons.

3 'Two wrongs don't make a right.' Is that a fair assessment of violent revolution, however just the cause may be (or seem)?

4 Some people believe our society can never be transformed. They therefore seek to try to undermine and destroy it so that a new society can be formed. Can you think of examples of such groups or people? Do you think society can be changed in such a way?

AUTHORITY IN RELIGION

From where do the different religions take their authority? On what are their claims for truth based?
● **The life and teaching of their founder** Jews look to the founding fathers of the nation—Abraham, the man of faith, Moses the law-giver. Christians, too, respect the authority of the 'Old Testament' law and prophets. But they look especially to Jesus—his life and teaching, the foundation of the 'new age' he came to inaugurate.
● **Sacred writings** The authority of the founder of a faith is transmitted by his writings. The *Qur'an* is the final authority for Muslims. In the case of Jesus, we have four accounts of his life ('Gospels') not *by* him but by his closest followers, plus the letters of the New Testament which explore the implications of his coming. Jesus also endorsed the writings of the Jewish Scriptures. So the Bible became the final authority and guide in all matters of faith and conduct for the Christian church.
● **Religious leaders** The different religions have built up a body of faith and teaching over the years, based on the teaching of religious leaders. Jewish teachers have given interpretations of the *Torah*, the Law. The Pope's official rulings add to the body of faith of the Roman Catholic Church. 'Tradition' may or may not be held by different groups to represent the work of the Holy Spirit in the church: Protestant Christians hold that the Bible alone is authoritative. Cults have often looked to their religious leader, especially to one with a particular spiritual experience.
● **Experience** Many religious groups have a strong tradition of the authority of the 'inner light' or mystical experience. Individual conscience has been seen as having authority in a person's life; or the leading of a group, perhaps through spiritual experience. The philosophy of 'existentialism' today stresses individual experience, and this has greatly influenced modern Christian and other movements. Guidance and the 'leading of the Holy Spirit' is a reality for the Christian: but one person's experience should not become an 'authority' or norm for others.

UNIT 14

MEDICINE

❛ Imagine a child born one hundred years after its father's death . . . human life spans doubled . . . weird hybrids, half-man and half-animal . . . genetic warfare . . . human reproduction without sex . . . control of mind, mood and memory by drugs. All are likely to come in the next few decades.❜

The last 150 years have witnessed amazing progress in the field of medicine. New drugs have been discovered which kill viruses and control pain. Diseases caused by poor standards of hygiene have been eliminated by improvements in sanitation and the public water supply. It has been possible to prevent some illnesses by inoculation and vaccination, and to control others by means of radiation. Modern engineering has made possible the production of spare parts for the human body, and of sophisticated machinery which assists doctors in both the diagnosis and the treatment of diseases.

A matter of life and death

The advances made by modern medicine have brought many areas of life and death under our control. But the achievements themselves—even while we may marvel at them—raise many moral and ethical questions.

The beginnings of life

As the way that the human body works has become more fully understood, it has become possible to prevent the birth of children.

● **Contraception** Contraception allows a man and woman to have sexual intercourse without risking

the conception of a child. Contraception can be practised by using the 'safe period' of the month when the woman cannot conceive. Modern medicine has developed more reliable methods: drugs and physical means of preventing conception.

Some people believe that reliable contraceptives are to be welcomed, because they result in *wanted* children, population control and the giving of dignity to human beings to decide whether or not their sexual union should result in a child. Others say that contraceptives

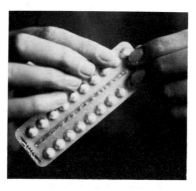

The oral contraceptive pill has provided an easy and reliable method of birth control. But not everyone agrees with its use.

interfere with the body's natural functions, lead to male selfishness and encourage promiscuity (casual sex).

● **Sterilization** Sterilization involves surgery, not normally reversible, which prevents the sperm and the egg from meeting. People who support sterilization do so because it dispenses with the use of contraceptives once a family is complete—desirable because of possible harmful side-effects of, say, the pill, on some women. Others, however, believe that sterilization goes too far in interfering with nature, and they are worried that some extremist governments might use it as a compulsory technique of population control.

● **Abortion** Abortion involves the ending of a baby's life after it has begun in the womb, but before birth. Carried out under careful medical supervision, an abortion is as 'safe' as

any other operation. Most abortions are performed before the twentieth week of pregnancy, before the baby actually makes its presence felt inside the mother.

Many of the arguments about abortion revolve around the point at which human life begins. Those in favour of abortion say that a woman should have the right to decide whether or not to continue with her pregnancy until the twentieth week. If she decides to terminate it (because of inability to cope, danger to her own life, rape, deformed baby, unplanned pregnancy, change of circumstances) she should be helped by the country's medical and social services.

Those who oppose abortion believe that a baby is a human being from

❛ It is difficult to kid yourself you are not taking life when you are throwing little arms, ribs and legs into a bucket.❜
Senior consultant

the moment of conception. It therefore has a right to live, especially as it cannot speak for itself. Opponents of abortion are also worried that easy abortion encourages immorality, carelessness and a devaluing of human life in general.

● **Genetic counselling** Some parents are persuaded not to have (more) children because there is a likelihood that the children born to them would be deformed or defective in some way. Enough is known about the minute elements of the sperm and egg cells, called genes, to be able to predict such occurrences, and this knowledge is used to counsel people against having children.

● **Infertility** Some couples (about one in ten) who want to be parents find that they are unable to have children. In some cases, medical science can help to discover why a baby is not being conceived. Sometimes it is possible to bring about conception by taking the husband's sperm and putting it into the woman (AIH: artificial insemination by husband). Most people would approve of this

WHAT ABOUT ABORTION?

'Life being a gift from God, a very sacred thing, abortion ought not to be entered into lightly, but after serious consideration of what is involved—the death of a potential human being. The Church of Scotland is opposed to abortion on demand, to abortion for purely social reasons, to the use of abortion as a means of birth control. The Church believes there are some areas where the termination of pregnancy is justified.
(1) If there is a risk of grave injury to the physical or mental health of the mother.
(2) In the case of proven rape.
(3) If there is certainty of a seriously defective child being born.'
The Church of Scotland

'. . . The regimen I adopt shall be for the benefit of the patients according to my ability and judgment, and not for their hurt or for any wrong. I will give no deadly drug to any, though it be asked of me, and especially I will not aid a woman to procure an abortion. Whatsoever house I enter there will I go for the benefit of the sick . . . Pure and holy will I keep my life and my art . . .'
The Hippocratic Oath, taken by all doctors

'Can abortion ever be right? Yes. There are some cases, very few in number, when the continued existence of the foetus will deny his mother her own right to life. In such a case, either the mother or the foetus must surrender the right to life; there is no other option. It is widely accepted that the life of the mother with her existing duties and obligations to her family is the more valuable. This view is strengthened by the fact that the apparent choice is illusory because the child is most unlikely to survive the death of the mother.

'Having once agreed that in the rare case, abortion is justified to save the life of the mother during pregnancy, it is illogical to refuse it in the case where the child after its birth would cripple the health of the mother and for all practical purposes, orphan her family. This granted, can abortion be denied to the mother who has not the emotional resources to cope with a further child and who will go to pieces with disastrous effects upon the welfare of her family?

'And so, step by step, the ground can be extended until we reach that point where only the contented, stable, affluent, healthy woman can be expected to proceed with her pregnancy! . . . The greatest problem in abortion is that of reaching a clear cut "yes" or "no" decision by assessing a number of factors: health, economic resources, prospects . . . none of which can be accurately measured and for none of which is there a generally accepted level of adequacy.'
Rex Gardner, consultant obstetrician

Healthy organs from a person who has died can sometimes be used as 'spare parts' for a sick person: transplants of kidneys and even hearts have become quite common, and it is possible to opt to donate organs for medical use should you suffer accidental death.

All kinds of problems are raised by these developments. Is the high cost of transplant operations justified? Do surgeons do such complicated operations to help people live, or to make a name for themselves? How should people whose lives might be saved by transplants be selected?

The end of life

Modern medicine and the increased understanding it has brought have had an effect upon the ending of life too.

● **Ageing** After the age of about forty-five, death occurs (apart from in accidents, war or natural disasters) either because parts of the body wear out, or because the body has been misused in such a way that disease destroys some essential organ. Transplant surgery (see above) has prolonged life for some in the first category, but knowledge of how to take care of themselves has also led many people to change their life-style.

If you are constantly tense and worried, working under pressure, if you eat too much of the wrong kind of food (such as starch or fats), if you do not take sufficient exercise and if you drink or smoke heavily, then your body will wear out more quickly or become diseased in some way.

● **Dying** Modern medicine can be used to 'control' death to some extent. If a person is severely injured in an accident, it is possible to keep his or her bodily functions going by means of a life-support machine. Whether the person is really 'living' or not, is something which a doctor has to decide before switching off the machine. Death is now normally defined as a state in which electrical activity in the brain has ceased.

Some wealthy people have tried to make arrangements to preserve their lives beyond death. They have paid for their bodies to be stored in ice, in the hope that while they are in that

method of bringing about conception, but there are many objections when the sperm of another man, or anonymous donor (AID) is used. This raises many social and legal questions, as well as moral and religious ones. Should the woman ever know the donor? Is the child 'legitimate'? Is AID a form of adultery? How will it affect the married couple's own relationship?

It is also possible to fertilize an egg outside the womb, allowing it to develop in a culture ('test-tube babies'). The embryo can then be implanted into the mother's (or any other woman's) womb to complete development. In the latter case, a 'surrogate mother' has the child for a woman unable to conceive or complete a pregnancy. But to whom does the child belong?

Preserving life

Lives are 'preserved' to a greater extent—that is, we live longer—than 100 years ago because of the improvements in medicine; there are fewer common illnesses which can kill us. Between the ages of four and forty-five, the commonest cause of death is accident—at work, on the roads or in sporting activities.

However, lives can now also be preserved by modern techniques in surgery. When a part of the body becomes diseased or worn out, it is sometimes possible to replace it with a manufactured spare part—plastic, metal or electronic. New joints can be put into our skeleton to help us move more easily, and plastic valves can be put into our hearts so that they continue to work properly.

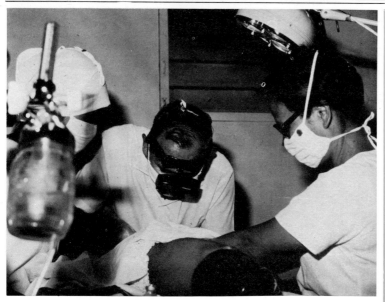

Christians have always been actively involved in caring for people through medical work. They see this as a way of showing God's love to people in need.

state, a cure for their disease will be discovered. Then they can be unfrozen, and the treatment given so that they can live again!

There are others who do not wish their lives to be prolonged: intense pain or an incurable illness may mean that they feel they would rather die by the withholding of drugs or treatment. This raises all kinds of questions about 'mercy-killing' which are considered in the next unit (Old Age).

Christians and medicine

Although it is hard to find agreement in detail between all the Christian churches on the ethical issues touched on in this unit, there is one over-riding principle which operates for Christians in the field of medicine. It is *compassion*—a form of love which acts to help people.

Christians are compassionate because they believe that God is compassionate—that his love prompts him to be helpful and merciful. Christians therefore make a conscious effort to model their lives upon Jesus, who came to earth to show what God is like. The way that Jesus treated people points to a God who is compassionate.

The Bible does not give detailed guidance on the many and complex medical issues which face us today, but there are certain principles which are applicable:

● **God and human life** Christians believe that every human life is sacred and of equal value to God. All control over life and death ultimately belongs to God. This means that great care must be taken with medical advances which tempt us to 'play God' and shape the future of the human race in some way. It also means that any development which devalues the individual (whether healthy or handicapped, old or unborn) must be strongly resisted.

On this basis, the Roman Catholic Church teaches that abortion, artificial insemination and any artificial means of contraception are wrong. Other Christians would not go along with such a blanket prohibition but would try to look at each situation according to biblical principles—the sanctity of life, the rights of the unborn child, responsible management of world resources and God's purposes for marriage and sex. They also believe that care and understanding should be shown to those who are caught in family or social dilemmas and who are trying to work out the right thing to do.

● **God and health** The health laws given by God to the Jews in the Old

'YOUR LIFE IN THEIR HANDS'

The questions raised by medical progress all stem from four groups of underlying principles. You may like to discuss some (or all) of these:

● **Purpose** What is medicine for? Should it aim to preserve life (make it *longer*) or improve life (make it *better*)? Should it do both?

● **Choice** Suppose five people need a kidney machine, but only one machine is available. How do you choose the lucky person? Should it be someone who is of the greatest value to the community? Do you choose an unskilled labourer or a highly-paid executive? Should limited hospital resources be used to help someone who has been deliberately careless with his life, such as a drug addict or reckless motor-cyclist? These sort of issues beg some of the most basic questions anyone can ask: Are all men equal? What is the value of a person? What am I here for?

● **Money** Limited resources throw problems of choice into even sharper focus. Should wealthy countries spend vast amounts on expensive machinery and equipment while poor countries cannot even afford the drugs which would save hundreds of people from easily preventible, common diseases? Should people who are well off be able to buy better treatment and facilities while those who are poorer, and those who choose to use their money in other ways, have a lower standard of medical care?

● **Responsibility** Should people be allowed to decide for themselves whether or not to join an insurance scheme to provide for their needs if they become ill, rather than be forced to contribute taxes to the National Health Service? Some people believe this should be a matter of personal responsibility, while others point out that such a system would leave poor and inadequate people with no choice at all. And what about laws making the wearing of crash helmets and seat belts compulsory? Should this be left to people's own sense of responsibility?

Testament are quite remarkable. Many of the principles which lie behind these laws were not 'rediscovered' until the nineteenth and twentieth centuries, despite being clearly set out in the Bible! The Jews were forbidden to eat certain foods which were unsafe in their climate. There were strict regulations about the safety of drinking water, the safe disposal of sewage, and the isolation of people with contagious diseases. If some of these laws had been followed in the UK at the time of the Industrial Revolution, many lives would have been saved.

Many people believe that God put these laws into the Jewish system to prevent sickness and to preserve their health. He is concerned that we look after our bodies and live in healthy and hygienic conditions.

● **God and healing** The Bible, particularly the New Testament, recounts examples of God's healing power over disease or paralysis. Jesus himself healed countless numbers of people, and sent his followers to do the same, as a demonstration that in the new creation, the new kingdom he had come to bring, illness and death would be no more. In the future this will be universal, when the whole universe has been 'made new' at the coming again of Jesus. In the meantime we still get ill, grow old and die—though the power of the kingdom in healing can still also be demonstrated today.

God has enabled man to discover many wonderful drugs and treatments which can cure a whole range of illnesses, and he can use those means to 'heal' people. And there are also examples of people who have been directly healed by God himself, without any medical intervention.

● **Death** Death is 'separation': separation of the life from the body, separation of people from one another; above all, separation of people from God. Because of human sin, we have shut ourselves out of God's presence. Illness, suffering and death are all part of this sinfulness, this 'fallen-ness', of human nature. This is why Jesus could come to 'die for our sins': to take the death, the separation from God, due to us. For the Christian who is trusting in Jesus, death becomes a gateway to a new world: the 'sting' of death has been taken away.

Discussion topics

1 Can you think of ways in which the control that medical science has

given us over birth, life and death could get out of hand and be misused? Does it matter? (Read Aldous Huxley's *Brave New World* for a glimpse of the sort of world that *could* result, and remember Hitler's idea of a 'master race'.)

2 Is contraception a social responsibility in the light of the world crisis of population and resources?

3 Under what circumstances (if any) do you think abortion should be allowed? Do you think there should be abortion on demand? Should the feelings of the doctors and nurses who have to perform and assist at the operation be taken into account?

4 Is there a difference between 'being alive' and 'living'? Why do you think people are so keen to preserve their lives for as long as possible? Are you afraid of dying?

5 In 1984 the Warnock Report (report of the committee of inquiry into human fertilization and embryology) was published. Among the recommendations were:
● AIH is acceptable.
● AID should be properly organized and licensed.
● AID children should be legitimate.
● AID children should have the right to know about the donor when 18 years old.
● In vitro fertilization should be available on NHS.
● Surrogate motherhood agencies should be banned because it is morally objectionable.
● Experiments on in vitro embryos to be allowed only for first two weeks.
● No human embryo which has been used for research can be implanted in a woman.
What are your views?

In vitro fertilization is the fertilization of an egg by a sperm in a test tube prior to transference of the egg to the woman.

Surrogate motherhood is where a woman has a baby, intending to pass it over to another woman when it is born.

UNIT 15

OLD AGE

'Joseph and Hannah Brown . . . appeared to be indestructible. For as long as I could remember they had lived together in the same house by the common. They had lived there, it was said, for fifty years; which seemed to me for ever. They had raised a large family and sent them into the world, and had continued to live on alone, with nothing left of their noisy brood save some dog-eared letters and photographs.

'The old couple were as absorbed in themselves as lovers, content and self-contained; they never left the village or each other's company, they lived as snug as two podded chestnuts. By day blue smoke curled up from their chimney, at night the red windows glowed; the cottage, when we passed it said "Here live the Browns", as though that were part of nature.

'Though white and withered, they were active enough, but they ordered their lives without haste. The old woman cooked, and threw grain to the chickens, and hung out her washing on bushes; the old man fetched wood and chopped it with a billhook, did a bit of gardening now and then, or just sat on a seat outside his door and gazed at the valley, or slept. When summer came they bottled fruit, and when winter came they ate it. They did nothing more than was necessary to live, but did it fondly, with skill—then sat together in their clock-ticking kitchen enjoying their half-century of silence . . .

'It seemed that the old Browns belonged for ever, and that the miracle of their survival was made commonplace by the durability of their love—if one should call it love, such a balance. Then suddenly, within the space of two days, feebleness took them both. It was as though two machines, wound up and synchronized, had run down at exactly the same time. Their interdependence was so legendary that we didn't notice their plight at first. But after a week, not having been seen about, some neighbours thought it best to call. They found old Hannah on the kitchen floor feeding her man with a spoon. He was lying in a corner half-covered with matting, and they were both too weak to stand. She had chopped up a plate of peelings, she said, as she hadn't been able to manage the fire. But they were all right really, just a touch of the damp; they'd do, and it didn't matter.

'Well, the Authorities were told; the Visiting Spinsters got busy; and it was decided they would have to be moved. They were too frail to help each other now, and their children were too scattered, too busy. There was but one thing to be done; it was for the best; they would have to be moved to the Workhouse.

'The old couple were shocked and terrified, and lay clutching each other's hands. "The Workhouse"—always a word of shame, grey shadow falling on the close of life, most feared by the old (even when called "The Infirmary"); abhorred more than debt, or prison, or beggary or even the stain of madness.

'Hannah and Joseph thanked the Visiting Spinsters but pleaded to be left at home, to be left as they wanted, to cause no trouble, just simply to stay together. The Workhouse could not give them the mercy they needed, but could only divide them in charity. Much better to hide, or die in a ditch or to starve in one's familiar kitchen, watched by the objects one's life had gathered—the scrubbed empty table, the plates and saucepans, the cold grate, the white stopped clock . . .

'"You'll be well looked after," the Spinsters said, "and you'll see each other twice a week." The bright busy voices cajoled with authority and the old couple were not trained to defy them. So that same afternoon, white and speechless, they were taken away to the Workhouse. Hannah Brown was put to bed in the Women's Wing, and Joseph lay in the Men's. It was the first time, in all their fifty years, that they had ever been separated. They did not see each other again, for in a week they were both dead.'

From *Cider With Rosie*, by Laurie Lee

An ageing population

When Laurie Lee wrote about Joseph and Hannah in *Cider With Rosie*, describing life in the Cotswold village of his childhood, he brought out two major aspects of old age.

One picture is of a 'golden age', with happy memories, comfortable companionship and a leisurely, peaceful life in familiar surroundings in the company of one's friends. The other is of failing strength and inability, the loss of independence, the threat of separation and institutionalization.

In many ways Joseph and Hannah were fortunate. They lived at the beginning of the twentieth century, when there were far fewer old people. There are now four times as many people over sixty-five in the UK than there were in 1900. As people live longer, the elderly are not only becoming more numerous, but they are forming a larger and larger *proportion* of the total population. At present, 13 per cent of the UK population is over sixty-five; in India the figure is 6 per cent, and in Brazil 3.5 per cent.

The problems of old age

● **Illness** As you grow older, you are subject to physical decline. Your body gets worn out through the natural process of ageing, and you probably develop typical 'old age illnesses' such as arthritis, bronchitis and circulation problems. Faculties such as sight and hearing become less sharp. All this leads to a loss of independence, a loss of confidence and a feeling of insecurity.

● **Poverty** Old people have to live on a reduced income. At sixty-five (or possibly younger for some), you are no longer allowed to work and receive a wage because you are thought to be too old. Some pensioners suffer a drop in their standard of living: they may not be able to provide sufficient food of the right kind, or sufficient warmth by way of clothes or fuel. Many old people cannot afford a telephone.

Many elderly people cannot afford adequate housing or adequate heating. They may feel lonely and isolated in a world that doesn't seem to need or want them.

FACTS AND FIGURES
Comparisons between the Western World and the Third World

	Western World	Third World
% of population over 65 in 1980:	11.4%	3.9%
Estimated % of population over 65 in 2000:	13.1%	4.6%
Estimated change in age group as a % of whole population between 1975 and 2075:		
Under 15	−22.0%	−52.0%
Over 65	+72.0%	+450.0%
Over 80	+153.0%	+900.0%

? Why do you think statisticians believe there will be a smaller number of children and larger numbers of old people in the future?

? What problems are likely to be encountered as a result of changes in population?

	1980	2000
Over 65 years old	258 million	396 million
Over 80 years old	26 million	60 million

? What do you notice about the birth-rates in the Third World compared to the West? What problems will this cause?

? Compare the percentage increases in the working population and the over-65 ('retired') age-group in the West. What problems will this create?

? Will the situation be worse or better in the Third World? Why?

? What characteristics of family life in Third World countries might help to ease the problem of so many old people?

In 1965, there were *ten* workers in the General Motors Corporation in the USA to support each pensioner from the firm. In 1979, the workforce had been reduced and the number of pensioners increased so that there were *four* workers for each pensioner. It has been calculated that by 1990 there will be *one* worker to each pensioner. This will result in vastly increased pension contributions, possibly rises of 300 per cent.

1965

1979

1990

They may also be frustrated because, while they have the time to visit people, to travel, to take up hobbies and to study, they may not have the money to do so. This can lead to another problem of old age . . .

● **Depression** The feeling of being a financial burden on the family or of intruding into the lives of others, the lack of visits to friends or interesting places, the knowledge that physical and mental powers are declining can combine to make old age a depressing and disappointing time.

One of the most important feelings for a human being is to feel wanted. Retirement—when a perfectly fit and able person is effectively told, 'Tomorrow, when you are sixty-five, you are not wanted here any more'—can be a real crisis. There can be the feeling that one is no longer valued for one's work in the community. Many a retired man's wife has to adjust to doing the same things each day but with a husband round the house, and only a fraction of the money each week to live on.

● **Loneliness** Old people who outlive their friends and/or spouses often find life very lonely. This can be particularly true for a widow or widower whose marriage was long and happy.

In the UK, 2.2 million old people live alone. They seldom have people of their own age to go and visit, and few younger people (even sometimes among their own families) think of visiting them. The death of friends and loved ones intensifies such feelings by emphasizing the nearness of death for them too.

'Loneliness' is more than just missing people—old people find that customs, places, money values, language and landmarks all change, and they miss the old ways with which they are familiar. A rapidly-changing world makes them feel confused and as if they do not belong.

Illness, poverty, depression and loneliness are often considered to be problems of old age—but in reality the problem lies outside these things. Old people are poor, they get depressed and lonely, only because of the way that society treats them. The root problem of the elderly is not biological ageing, but neglect and poor social conditions. Even the attitude that old people 'cannot do what they used to' can sometimes be true just because old people have got it into their heads that it is true.

When old people look at our society, they find that youth, glamour, physical prowess and material possessions are the things which are valued, and because they are limited in these areas, they feel that they are unimportant and that society does not value them. Even calling an elderly man 'Grandad' in a jocular fashion gives the impression that he is not to be taken seriously, and it can be hurtful.

Old people are not simply 'old people'—even though we have had to use that term in this unit. Each one is an individual in his/her own right. They have knowledge and experience built up over a lifetime, even though this is not valued a great deal in Western countries. Clearly, if old people are to be helped, it is not just the poverty and the ill-health which need attention, but attitudes towards old people have to be changed too.

'Help the aged'

There are two major ways in which old people can be helped or looked after in our society.

● **Family care** Parents normally sacrifice a lot for their children during the best years of their lives—they give time, money and energy to provide for them. When the parents are old, their children in turn have the opportunity to care for *them*. Many people believe that this is the best way to care for the elderly.

Some families make this possible by having the old person actually living with them, sometimes with a room or flat of their own so that they can feel independent and the family can still enjoy some privacy. If an old person can cope alone and wants to be completely independent of their family, they can be visited regularly in their own home; or, they may be settled in sheltered housing or an old people's home. Whatever the arrangement, the important thing is that old people feel that they are wanted, loved and respected by their families.

All too often in modern Western society this does not happen. In other cultures, however, the attitude to the old is very different. For a Muslim or Hindu, it is almost unthinkable that old people could be left to look after themselves, and, for this reason, very few people from these communities are found in old people's homes or geriatric wards. In some non-Western societies, the old enjoy great honour and esteem, and often wield considerable power in the family.

● **Community care** Not all old people have a family. Not all families can afford to look after their elderly relatives. Responsibility for the care

of old people, therefore, needs to be spread wider than the family.

The most extensive form of community care in the UK is provided by the government, via a state pension and a pension supplement (if the ordinary pension is not adequate). Other forms of state aid are the provision of cheaper (or free) public transport, council-funded old people's homes, sheltered housing and day centres, and attempts to meet personal needs by the 'meals on wheels' and 'home help' services.

Government provision can be very impersonal and, in any case, the help meets only material needs. The best form of community care is when the elderly are cared for by people in the local community whom they know and trust. Sometimes a local doctor co-ordinates various types of help: he can send someone to hospital if needed, or arrange for the district nurse to call and make sure that laundry and heating are attended to. This kind of provision is costly and is very unequal across the UK. Sometimes local people organize themselves on a voluntary basis to provide community care, and national charities often support efforts of this kind.

WHAT THE BIBLE SAYS

The Bible takes it for granted that old people will be cared for within the family, because the pattern of family life in Bible times was built around the 'extended family' (see Unit 3, The Family). There is therefore very little by way of specific commandment to look after the old. The emphasis in both the Old and New Testaments is on the need to *respect* old people, and certain guidelines are laid down:

'"Respect your father and mother, so that you may live a long time in the land that I am giving you."' (Exodus 20:12)
This is the fifth of the Ten Commandments.

★ ★ ★

'"Whoever curses his father or his mother is to be put to death."' (Exodus 21:17)

Nothing to do with bad language— this means leaving parents to the disposal (in the care) of the gods— i.e. God laid down severe punishment for failing to fulfil family responsibilities.

★ ★ ★

'"Show respect for old people and honour them."' (Leviticus 19:32)
Old people outside the family are to be treated with care and respect too.

★ ★ ★

[Jesus said] 'You have a clever way of rejecting God's law in order to uphold your own teaching. For Moses commanded, "Respect your father and your mother," and "Whoever curses his father or his mother is to be put to death." But you teach that if a person has something he could use to help his

father or mother, but says, "This is Corban" (which means, it belongs to God), he is excused from helping his father or mother.' (Mark 7:9–12)
Jesus told the Pharisees that to deny help to your family using the excuse of religious duty is hypocrisy, not devotion to God.

★ ★ ★

'If a widow has children or grandchildren, they should learn first to carry out their religious duties towards their own family and in this way repay their parents and grandparents, because that is what pleases God . . . If anyone does not take care of his relatives, especially the members of his own family, he has denied the faith and is worse than an unbeliever.' (1 Timothy 5:4, 8)

'The right to die'?

When people are near the end of life, either through great age or terminal illness (or both), wouldn't the kindest thing be to allow them to opt to die, to ask a doctor to put them out of their misery? This is what is known as voluntary euthanasia.

The word 'euthanasia' literally means 'gentle and easy death', but it has gradually come to be the term for 'mercy killing' or 'assisted suicide'. In 1936, the House of Lords debated a bill which proposed that patients should be allowed to request euthanasia if their illness was incurable, fatal and painful. It was designed to help doctors when they could no longer relieve the pain. The bill was rejected. In 1969, the House of Lords debated the Voluntary Euthanasia Bill which would have allowed a person to indicate their wish for euthanasia in advance of incurable and painful illness. Again, the bill was rejected.

The idea behind this was that people have a 'right to die' if it is the only way of ending suffering or preserving human dignity. Those who support voluntary euthanasia do so because they believe that:
● it is part of human freedom to be able to make this choice;
● the patient is released from painful suffering and a useless existence;
● it is harsh and unloving to make someone stay alive against their will;
● it is a final act of love towards loved ones, who would otherwise have to watch helplessly as death approached, and who may be suffering great strain and hardship in caring for the invalid;
● it relieves society of the burden of a person who is totally unproductive and expensive to look after.

Although these reasons sound compassionate, there are many (equally compassionate) people who are strongly opposed to euthanasia on the following grounds:
● **It is unnecessary** When the original bill was before parliament in 1936, a person could die in agony or in an undignified way because the means were not always available to relieve pain. This no longer applies. Drugs called analgesics are not only pain-killers, but they also relieve the tension of a terminal illness such as cancer. Often a person with only a short time to live is able to remain active, calm and conscious until they die.
● **Mistakes can happen** Doctors who have pronounced patients incurable have sometimes been mistaken. Dr Christian Barnard of South Africa once described a night when he decided to end a patient's life. The woman was in agony, dying because she had a growth in her womb. She sobbed and screamed, and bit Barnard's hand as he put it over her mouth to quieten her. He went out for more morphine which would put her to sleep—permanently. When he returned, she was asleep, and something stopped him from giving the fatal injection. She woke up next morning feeling much better, and after six weeks, she left the hospital free of pain.

There are aspects of illness which are still not fully understood. Sometimes there is complete recovery from what seems to be a fatal, painful illness.

❛ A society's health must be judged by the way it treats its weakest members.❜
David Field, lecturer, theologian and author

● **Is the patient 'in his right mind'?** If a person signs a form to say that his life is to be ended if he is terminally ill or senile, is he in his right mind when he signs the statement? Can he understand what he will feel like when he is too ill or too old to speak? If someone is *already* suffering distress, is it a rational decision or could they be prompted to sign by the stress of the moment?
● **There could be unfair pressure** Many people believe that if euthanasia were legalized, old people might be 'encouraged' to ask for it. An old person living with a family in a small house, whose illness is causing strain, might be put under pressure and feel that 'being put to sleep' would be the best solution for everyone's benefit.
● **The thin end of the wedge** If euthanasia were allowed for the

ORGANIZED HELP

Individual, family and community care cannot cover *all* the needs of elderly people in our society. There are many organizations seeking to help, of which three of the best known are:
● **Age Concern** (Bernard Sunley House, 60 Pitcairn Road, Mitcham, Surrey CR4 3LL)
This co-ordinates over 1,000 local efforts to help old people in the UK. Local groups operate visiting schemes, transport to hospital and social activities, holidays, day trips, form-filling and fetching prescriptions. About 60,000 home visits are made each year. Headquarters provides the support for local groups, prepares reports on old people for local and central government and other bodies, and publishes a quarterly magazine. It acts as a pressure group and sets up its own projects. The Department of Health and Social Security gives a small grant, but the rest of the money needed comes from voluntary donations.
● **The National Corporation for the Care of Old People** (Nuffield Lodge, Regents Park, London NW1 4RS)
This was set up in 1947—as a result of a report by the Nuffield Foundation—to continue to carry out study and research, and to use funds to start experimental services which would help old people. The corporation has looked at housing needs in retirement, social and welfare services for the elderly at home. It is financially supported by charitable trusts and foundations.
● **Help the Aged** (32 Dover Street, London W1A 2AA)
This is a Christian-based international charity launched in 1962 because of the realization that many people would willingly give money if the needs of the elderly were only presented clearly enough. It became a large fund-raising organization using gift shops, advertising and collections, and as a result has been able to give grants to many welfare projects around the world. It started the Anchor Housing Association in the UK, and gives help to old people overseas when they suffer because of natural disasters or political upheavals. Grants are channelled through relief teams, churches, the Red Cross and the United Nations Organization. Help the Aged publishes its own newspaper and provides literature for schools.

THE HOSPICE MOVEMENT

The problems of old age, senility and incurable or painful illness will be with us long after the dust has settled on the arguments for or against voluntary euthanasia. What positive contribution can be made to ease the suffering caused by these tragic human situations? One Christian response has been the founding and development of the hospice movement for the care of the terminally ill.

A 'hospice' is literally a 'house of rest for travellers', but in the context of the hospice movement, it has come to mean a place where terminally ill patients can receive individual, caring treatment from staff trained in both medicine and counselling. Pain is controlled, and the dying patient is prepared mentally and spiritually for death, which is seen as the end of their illness but the start of a new life. Members of the patient's family are also included in this preparation.

This compassionate caring for the dying is based on the Christian belief that every human life matters. Cecily Saunders, the founder of the movement, says that only a very small number of patients have wanted to discuss euthanasia; once their pain and feeling of isolation had been relieved, they never asked again.

senile, incurably ill and those in great pain, why not for the handicapped, habitual criminals or any group the government of the day considered a threat or a burden? It might only be a matter of time before euthanasia was extended to other groups of people. Opponents claim that this is exactly what happened in Germany under the Nazis, who practised compulsory euthanasia on over 6 million Jews. Extermination of individuals against their will is immoral and should never be allowed to happen again.

● **It would destroy the doctor/patient relationship** If patients thought that their doctor sometimes 'killed' people because there was no cure for their illness, or because their pain could not be alleviated, this could seriously affect the relationship of trust which must exist between doctor and patient. As the law stands at present, a doctor who helped a person to die would in any case be acting illegally: suicide is not illegal, but assisting someone to commit suicide is.

● **It is against God's law** Most Christians would hold to the reasons against voluntary euthanasia described above, but would regard them as *supportive* arguments only. The crunch issue for them is that life is a gift from God, and that every individual is made with the potential for a relationship with God. We can never write anyone off as 'useless' or a 'human vegetable' if we believe this.

Christians also believe that *real* compassion is shown by deep loving and caring for the sick and suffering, and that the sacrifice involved strengthens character and is never 'wasted effort'. They believe that God's strength is available even in the most difficult situations, and that God has a purpose for each individual life. To ask for euthanasia would be to deny some of the fundamentals of the Christian faith.

Discussion topics

1 Someone has said that the twentieth-century attitude towards old people ought to be called 'Ageism' so that it could be recognized as an evil, like 'Racism'. Do you agree?

2 What problems would be created (for *everyone* concerned) if an elderly relative moved in with your family? How would you try to resolve them?

3 What is your attitude to growing old? Do you think that fear is a factor in discrimination against the elderly?

EDUCATION

How often have you heard someone say, after seeing or experiencing something new—'Well, you live and learn'? In one sense, learning is living. When you were a baby, you learned to sit up and then to crawl, walk and climb. You learned to speak, to recognize sounds and voices.

Learning is something you cannot *help* doing. When you see something new, you remember it, and it becomes part of what you know. When something happens which

LIVING AND LEARNING IN AN AFRICAN MUSLIM VILLAGE

❛ Adults passing anywhere near the children would solemnly pretend not to see or hear as Sitafa, Kunta, and the rest of their *kafo* growled and roared like lions, trumpeted like elephants, and grunted like wild pigs, or as the girls—cooking and tending their dolls and beating their *couscous*—played mothers and wives among themselves. But however hard they were playing, the children never failed to pay every adult the respect which their mothers had taught them to show always toward their elders. Politely looking the adults in the eyes, the children would ask "*Kerabe?*" (Do you have peace?) And the adults would reply "*Kera dorong*". (Peace only.) And if an adult offered his hand, each child in turn would clasp it with both hands, then stand with palms folded over his chest until that adult passed by.

'Kunta's home-training had been so strict that, it seemed to causes pleasure or pain, you 'remember for next time'. You can learn by being told and by discovering things for yourself.

Learning seems to be so basic and important to us as human beings that it has been suggested that we have something inside us which makes us long for knowledge and experience, and hate boredom. We therefore make efforts to keep on learning.

Learning can be much more than living. Learning takes place when someone sets out to teach us things we would not normally experience for ourselves. Our parents may tell us stories which are part of our national heritage and culture. We also learn from them our place in the community, what is expected of us and how we should behave. We are taught what our parents and our society believe is right and wrong, and we may also be taught the religious beliefs and practices which our parents follow.

In more primitive communities, children learn from their parents how to survive and how to look after themselves, how to use weapons, build homes and grow food. This is still the means of passing on skills and knowledge in many parts of the developing world.

Formal education

Education conducted at home was adequate as long as the life of society remained fairly simple. But as it became more complex in many parts of the world, the need for education outside the family became obvious.

There were four major developments which led to this change.

● **Development of skills** As new skills were needed to keep pace with developments in commerce and technology, parents found that they could not teach their children what was needed. England in the sixteenth century had a strong apprentice system which developed to teach boys a trade; in the same period, schools such as Eton and St Paul's were set up to train children for

❨ Every child shall be given an education which will promote his general culture and enable him on a basis of equal opportunity to develop his abilities, his individual judgment and his sense of moral and social responsibility and to become a useful member of society. ❩
United Nations Declaration of the Rights of a Child

posts in the church and in government. After the Industrial Revolution, jobs became more specialized and the same person rarely saw a job through from beginning to end. New service industries—communications, banking —came into being for which parents had no training. It soon became necessary for all children to learn the 'three R's': reading, writing and arithmetic. Many were also taught how to operate machinery.

● **Development of knowledge** The rediscovery of printing in the West in the fifteenth century and the changeover to popular usage of local languages such as English and French instead of the 'official' languages of Latin and Greek set in motion a positive 'explosion' of knowledge. Suddenly it became possible to get to know all that had been learned up to that point. Scientific method was used to discover more about the world. The amount of knowledge now available is so great that, even with printing and modern methods of communication, it is difficult to keep up with new developments even in a general way. Parents can no longer keep up with all there is to know.

So a broad education is attempted by professional teachers outside the home and inside a school. However, with the amount of knowledge in the world doubling every ten years, even teachers find it difficult to keep pace with developments in their subjects!

---

him, his every move drew Binta's irritated finger-snapping—if, indeed, he wasn't grabbed and soundly whipped. When he was eating he would get a cuff on the head if Binta caught his eyes on anything except his own food. And unless he washed off every bit of dirt when he came into the hut from a hard day's play, Binta would snatch up her scratchy sponge of dried plant stems and her bar of homemade soap and make Kunta think she was going to scrape off his very hide.

'For him ever to stare at her, or at his father, or at any other adult, would earn him a slap as quickly as when he committed the equally serious offence of interrupting the conversation of any grown-up. And for him to speak anything but truth would have been unthinkable. Since there never seemed any reason for him to lie, he never did.

'Though Binta didn't seem to think so, Kunta tried his best to be a good boy, and soon began to practice his home-training lessons with the other children. When disagreements occurred among them, as they often did— sometimes fanning into exchanges of harsh words and finger-snapping—Kunta would always turn and walk away, thus displaying the dignity and self-command that his mother had taught him were the proudest traits of the Mandinka tribe.

'But almost every night, Kunta got spanked for doing something bad to his baby brother—usually for frightening him by snarling fiercely, or by dropping on all fours like a baboon, rolling his eyes, and stomping his fists like forepaws upon the ground. "I will bring the *toubob*!" Binta would yell at Kunta when he had tried her patience to the breaking point, scaring Kunta most thoroughly, for the old grandmothers spoke often of the hairy, red-faced, strange-looking white men whose big canoes stole people away from their homes. ❩
From *Roots*, by Alex Haley

❓ How many different kinds of 'education' are mentioned in this extract?
❓ What methods were used to teach the Mandinka children how to behave?
❓ Can you think of modern Western equivalents in each case?

Education is a prized commodity in many developing countries. Here, students in Botswana find out their examination results. Only one-third of those completing primary school will be able to continue to secondary school because educational provision is limited.

● **Increase of population** Between 1801 and 1970, the population of the UK increased by over 40 million, rising from 15 million to 55 million. The rapid increase in population in the mid-nineteenth century gave rise to squalid and crowded living conditions in the manufacturing towns. There was a great deal of crime, disease and poverty. Many people began to believe that the best way of solving the social problems was through education, as parents in such situations could not cope with teaching their large families. At the same time, the 'middle classes' believed that those who were working in the factories needed to be educated into punctuality and discipline!

● **Increase in mobility** This 'mobility' may take different forms. In the literal sense of movement and travel, new forms of transport and communication have made the world a smaller place. It has become necessary to learn foreign languages and to understand different cultures, in order to avoid misunderstanding and prejudice. Another recent change is that people no longer live in the same place all their lives. Parents' work may involve them in travel, which makes it impossible for them to educate their own children.

There is also something known as 'social mobility'. As a general rule, parents want their children to enjoy opportunities which they themselves were denied in their youth. 'A good education' is seen as a good start in life and may also mean that their children can try for jobs which will move them up the 'social ladder'.

This has led to a demand by parents for a sound, formal education as a 'right'—they recognize that they themselves cannot give their children the necessary education.

However, the fact that education in our kind of society needs to take place outside home does not mean that parents should give up *all* aspects of educating their children. There may be the temptation to put total responsibility on to the school. Ideally, the home is still the best place for health and sex education, moral and religious education.

Once a government becomes involved in education (what we now call 'the state system'), it has to be responsible for the maintenance of certain standards:

● Standards of education have to be seen to be equal throughout the country.

● Teachers must all be trained to be able to teach to an acceptable standard.

● The quality of education given in all schools must reach a standard which can be tested by an examinations system.

● Regulations have to ensure that all children go to school for a minimum number of days each year.

● Sufficient books and materials must be provided.

● School buildings must meet certain fixed standards.

If parents believe that some or all

GOVERNMENT INVOLVEMENT IN EDUCATION

1870 All schools put under authority of bodies called School Boards. Children aged 5–12 years old could attend.

1876 Every parent had to make sure that their child(ren) had elementary education in reading, writing and arithmetic. Children could leave school when they reached a required standard in these skills.

1880 All children up to 10 years old had to attend school. School Boards could enforce attendance.

1902 Local Education Authorities came into being, all schools in one area coming under the appropriate Authority. Children had to be given the chance to receive secondary education (i.e. more advanced than elementary) and scholarships could be given to make up for loss of wages.

1918 School-leaving age raised to 14. LEAs now responsible for education from 3 to 16. Day Continuation Schools set up for 14–16 year olds.

1944 All children now had to receive secondary education, in grammar, technical or modern schools.

1976 All state secondary schools obliged by law to become comprehensive (non-selective) schools.

1986 Government promotion of new 16 + examination, the General Certificate of Secondary Education (GCSE) and proposal to assess all teachers.

of these standards are not being met at a certain state school, they can talk the matter over with the headteacher. As a last resort, they can contact a school governor or the local education authority.

A state system is obviously open to abuse by the government which ultimately controls it. A government may manipulate the education system to fit its own political aims—whether these are the maintenance of one-party control, the provision of equal opportunity or the supply of trained workers for particular jobs.

But . . .

Even though the state system is accepted by most people—because a voluntary system or education by parents clearly could not cope—it raises many important questions. What do you think are the answers?

● **What is the best size for a school?** In a big school, there are generally better facilities such as

EDUCATION AND WORLD FAITHS

Religion was probably the most important sponsor of education before the state realized its importance.

In India, education was formerly reserved for the upper castes because of cost, and took place in the home of the teacher, or *guru*. Students learned the sacred books and hymns of **Hinduism** by heart.

In modern Hinduism, the aim of life is to achieve a state of salvation where there is no need to be reborn into this life. Education is therefore designed to give that knowledge of God which will lead to salvation. Subjects such as history and geography are windows through which one sees the whole of life, and this leads to knowledge of self and knowledge of God. The aim of Hindu education is to help a child to realize his duty, his responsibilities and his obligations to others.

Religion is important in education in **Islam**. Religious and moral education are at the heart of the curriculum. Father teaches 'the revealed word of God' at home, but all boys also attend school at the mosque from about the age of four to learn to read and recite passages from the *Qur'an*. They also study the law, religion and themes such as marriage and inheritance.

Teachers are always treated with great respect. Girls also learn about the *Qur'an*, but they are taught by their mothers at home. In Islam, the purpose of education is to contribute to the community: 'I will do those things which will benefit others.'

The Bible gives examples of the ways in which **Jewish** children were taught. In the Old Testament, children learned the laws of God and Jewish religious history and customs from their parents. A boy would learn his trade from his father; a girl learned spinning and weaving from her mother. Education for all aspects of life was completely within the family.

By the time of Jesus, most synagogues had a school attached, where boys were taught by rabbis; they learned the Jewish scriptures by heart. On his first day at school, the Jewish boy went with his father to have breakfast with his teacher. He was given small cakes to eat which had texts from the scriptures inscribed on them—to impress on him that the purpose of his education was to get the scriptures inside him! The home was still the place where trades and skills were taught. For example, Jesus learned carpentry because his earthly father, Joseph, was a carpenter.

---

libraries, craft rooms and sports areas, because these can be provided more economically for a large number of pupils, say 1,500–2,000. However, individual pupils may feel 'lost' in such a complex organization. The personal touch is missing and they feel they do not matter. How do we achieve the right balance?

● **Is there really such a thing as 'equal opportunity'?** In 1944, 'equal opportunity' meant that everyone was taught in equivalent buildings with similar provision of equipment, even though the schools were divided into grammar, technical and modern. Later, 'equal opportunity' came to mean that everyone should have a fair chance of getting to a grammar school. Many people now believe that 'equal opportunity' means giving children from different backgrounds the same education and therefore the same start in life. What does it really mean?

● **How should pupils be assessed?** Many people do not like the examination system because they believe it has too much influence on what is studied in schools, and because it tests in two hours a whole course of work which may have taken up to two years to complete. Some pupils react very badly to exams and do not do themselves justice. But prospective employers or higher education institutions have to have some standard and recognized measure of applicants' abilities. Is there a way of producing school reports or assessments which are fair, useful and valuable? Should a pupil's achievement be assessed in relation to his own ability, or compared with a national standard (as in public examinations)?

● **Should a school be part of the local community?** Some schools are only open for pupils between 9 o'clock and 4 o'clock, and parents only visit for parents' evenings and school functions. In other places, the school runs a playgroup, and local youth groups, evening classes and higher education groups use the facilities after school hours. Is it a good idea to use schools in this way? Should school students be involved in local community service projects?

● **Should schools prepare pupils for work?** The Technical and Vocational Education Initiative (TVEI) started in 1983 in fourteen areas of the UK. It is run for fourteen to eighteen year olds by the Manpower Services Commission. The course details are decided by local education authorities but the courses must give equal opportunities for both sexes, prepare students for employment in a rapidly-changing society, have technical and vocational elements related to local job opportunities as well as general ones, give work experience from age fifteen, and develop problem-solving skills and initiative. The Certificate of Pre-Vocational Education (CPVE) is a one-year course for people staying on for a year after sixteen. It includes core studies (such as personal and career development, numeracy, science and technology, and practical skills), vocational studies with at least fifteen days on-the-job work experience (such as business and administrative services, technical services, production, distribution and services to people) and additional studies to provide time for 'community activities, leisure, recreation and reflection'.

● **Do schools prepare pupils for life?** Do current social trends among young people—increase in juvenile crime, drug abuse, vandalism and drunkenness—indicate that the schools have failed? Do schools take away the opportunity for pupils to make their own decisions, practise self-discipline and be prepared for 'real life' outside school? Is life experience more important than learning facts? Can it be 'taught'?

● **What should be learned?** Some schools are accused of putting so many subjects such as health education, political education, careers and preparation for parenthood on the timetable that competence in the basic essentials (which is still required by employers) is put at risk. Which are more important? Some pupils are allowed to take commerce or a second language; others are not given this chance. Is this fair?

Schools also 'teach' through school clubs, streaming, reception of visitors, rules, the punishment system, extra work, support for charities, status, relationships in the school and the pastoral system—none of which is on the timetable. What do you learn from these? Are they important?

● **What kind of religious education should there be?**
Religion is such an important part of the world scene, and so bound up with history and culture, that it must feature in the education system. Some people say that we should know about Christianity in depth; others say that we should learn about all the major religions, so that we begin to understand what religion is all about. Who is right?

Christianity and education

Since the Middle Ages, and in many of the developing countries today, the church has played an important role in education. It has had the motivation (concern for people), premises (church property) and people (the clergy) who could teach.

Why are Christians so interested in education?
● Christianity's origins were in Judaism, and the Jews had a very strong tradition of education—both in the family and at the synagogue schools.
● Christians believe that every individual is important and that each person's talents and abilities are gifts from God which should be developed. Education can help someone to achieve their God-given potential.
● A knowledge of Christianity is vital to an informed understanding of much of Western history and culture.
● Concern about injustice and inequality has led Christians to be involved in providing educational opportunities for those who might otherwise be neglected.
● Many Christians see teaching as a 'vocation'—a person-to-person job which God has called them to do so

that they can apply Christian beliefs about relationships, unselfish attitudes, corporate life and institutions to their work.
● Christianity gives people a motive for becoming literate and informed. Jesus commanded his disciples to 'go into all the world and preach the gospel'. For people to have the opportunity of finding out what the Bible says, how to become Christians and to live as God wants them to, they need to be able to read for themselves.
● Christianity is concerned with personal relationships. It therefore has a lot more to teach than 'just information'—attitudes to myself, to other people as well as to God. It can be said to be part of 'education for life' and is a sound basis for moral education.

Discussion topics

1 Some educational experts (called 'de-schoolers') believe that education should be related to experiences that we have rather than facts that we learn. The important question is 'What things and people do learners wish to have contact with?' not 'What facts do we need to know in order to be educated?' Do you agree? Is it a case of either/or, or can there be a balance?
2 If you were designing a school timetable to be of maximum use to you in *all* areas of life, what would a typical week's (or fortnight's) programme look like?
3 In modern society, where would you draw the line between the responsibilities of home and school in education?
4 Do you think that fee-paying schools should be abolished or retained?
5 Over the last few years, so-called 'Free Schools' have been established, where the pupils are left to discipline themselves and discover for themselves the information they want to know. What do you think are the advantages and disadvantages of such a system?
6 Should religious education be compulsory? If so, how should it be taught? Can you have moral education without religious education?

WORK

Believe it or not, man was made for work! And work was a pleasure until human sinfulness spoiled it all . . .

Today we are having to think hard about the role of work in society. If there is not enough work for everyone, what are we going to do? What is going to be our contribution to the community? How are we going to fill our lives?

Craft or factory?

Work is based on sharing the jobs of the community round the members of that community. Instead of each home baking its own bread, one member of the community bakes the bread, another makes clothes, another teaches the children, and so on. Work is our basic 'employment': the way we employ our time to keep ourselves—and others—alive and fulfilling our purpose in the world.

This may seem a far cry from boring factories or desk jobs . . . How has the change come about?

At a time when communities were small and transport difficult, it made sense to keep work local. Agriculture was the main 'industry'. In 1851, 22 per cent of the population still worked on the land; by 1970, this had gone down to only 4 per cent.

The difference was, of course, better tools: one man with a tractor could produce what previously needed several men. It was one of the results of the Industrial Revolution. Power from water and steam, later electricity and oil, made it possible to 'mass produce'. Instead of work being done locally by craftsmen, goods could be manufactured more cheaply and efficiently if produced by large machinery.

Today our community is not the village, not even one country or one economic community, but the world. One multi-national company makes clothes, another electronics, another shoes . . . If we can get the balance right between what should be produced locally (e.g. bread) and what should be produced on a world-wide basis (e.g. cars), there is no reason why the world of work should not go on as before . . .

Technology

The Industrial Revolution was violently opposed when it was first introduced. Workers smashed the new machines which were taking their jobs. But the new technology created far more jobs than it took away. It created the whole new world of manufacturing industry, calling for skills in production, marketing, selling, accounting and many other areas.

In the same way we are fearful today of the impact of the 'electronic revolution'. The micro-chip is taking jobs—such as assembly-line jobs which can be done by computer-controlled robots, office jobs in which computers can do accounting and word processing. But again, the new technology is creating whole new industries. It makes it possible to do things we could not do at all before. It is too soon to see the overall impact on jobs. But already whole new areas are opening up for employment—in communications, information processing, production control, and so on. Will the micro-chip revolution and digital technology create more jobs than they have taken away?

Organizing work

Different types of organization have proved best for different types of jobs:

● **Self-employed** Many people run their own small businesses, such as shops, putting up the money or borrowing it, paying the expenses such as rent for premises; 'take-home pay' tends to be what is left, which of course can be a little or a lot, depending on how much a person can afford to take out of the business. In industries such as building contracting, companies prefer not to have a lot of people on the payroll. Instead, they hire people for a particular job. The self-employed person has to pay his own tax and National Insurance. And, of course,

there is no continuity of work or security. But he can be flexible. He is his own boss.

● **Partnership** Get together with one or more people and you have a partnership. Firms of accountants or solicitors, for instance, are often partnerships, pooling resources to make a more effective business.

● **Limited company** When a business gets bigger, the bills get so big that people's families and homes could be put at risk, so they form a company with 'limited liability': the company becomes something separate from them as individuals. Companies with 'Ltd' after their name in Britain are private limited companies—owned by a family or several people who 'share' ownership, i.e. 'shareholders'.

● **Public Limited Company** A company which has more than fifty shareholders, i.e. one whose shares are offered for sale to the general public, is a 'public' company. People who have money can put it to work by investing it in a public company. The 'stock exchanges' have been set up to 'exchange' (buy or sell) 'stock' (shares in companies) so that people can readily acquire shares or sell them if they need the money back. Companies needing money in order to grow pay the shareholders for the use of their money by paying a

'dividend'. If you have been left some money by Aunt Matilda, you may not have the skills yourself to work in, say, electronics, but by buying a share in an electronics company you are putting your money to productive use: you are investing it in electronics and so giving jobs to others.

● **Employee-owned companies** The snag, of course, with most companies is that it is the people who work for a company who are really its 'members'—the shareholders may not be involved at all, apart from their money. So companies are now introducing schemes to ensure that all employees are shareholders. Another way of doing this is not to have outside shareholders at all. A *co-operative* is a company where the people who work for it have put in the money equally.

● **Groups and multi-nationals** Many companies belong to a 'group' of companies, either within one country or internationally. Sometimes groups are formed to share resources: distribution, or accounting functions, or sales promotion; or simply to share financial resources.

● **Nationalized companies** If it is thought necessary for the country to own certain activities itself in the public interest, they are

TRADES UNIONS

One person on his (or her) own can be powerless. Get together with others and you get the strength of numbers. Trades unions were started from a Christian concern for people who were being exploited by greedy employers: people being given bad wages or working in bad conditions.

The unions have proved successful in achieving their aims. They have won proper wages for their members. They have improved working conditions. They have made an immense contribution to industry and commerce.

In Britain unions are organized according to type of job, not according to company. This means that clerical workers are in competition with manual workers, for instance, within one company. Whereas a company has to balance different needs in deciding

wages (the need to be in business next year as well as this, for instance), the union has only one factor to consider: the interests of its own membership. This can, of course, be ruthlessly selfish and lead to disruption and strikes.

Elsewhere, such as Japan, unions are organized by company, not type of job. This means that workers are also concerned for the future of their company.

In communist countries, the idea of unions is against the basic idea that the state represents the people. The people, therefore, own the means of production, so there's no need for a union of workers to represent them as well. Recent events in Poland, however, show otherwise. When the state becomes something different from the people, the result is oppression.

'nationalized': e.g. the railways once had separate companies for the different parts of the country; to co-ordinate the railways as one network they are now owned by the state. The debate about whether industries should be nationalized depends on whether a state monopoly or competition is thought better; whether the community should get the benefit from ownership—e.g. of oil or coal—as well as have the costs.

● **Collectives** Some communist countries have extended the idea of 'nationalized' or state ownership of industry to many other activities, such as farming. A co-operative is owned by the people who work for it. But a collective is owned by the state, run for the people as a whole.

Attitudes to work

There are as many different attitudes to work as there are people. Some are as follows:

● **Boring necessity** Work is just a way of earning your bread. The real thing in life is home or leisure time or holiday or the family or girls . . .

● **Job satisfaction** What's important in life is to do something worthwhile. There is satisfaction in doing a job well—helping to create a good product, or make a good sale, for instance. There is also job satisfaction in being part of a group doing something together.

● **Selling your labour** Rather than being part of a company of people achieving something, many working people have seen themselves as simply selling their labour to the highest bidder. The idea really belongs back with the Industrial Revolution. But many trades unions have continued it. So never mind what product the company is making, or whether it makes a profit or anything else, what is important is that *I* (or my union) get(s) the best deal for *me*.

● **Crafts and skills** People have different skills. Some are good at intricate work with their hands. Others are good at selling, or

❛ People will only be committed if they feel that their contribution matters. Nobody can care much about their work if they feel their jobs are not worthwhile. Huge organizations can make communication difficult and increasing specialization can make jobs dull, boring and repetitive. At the same time, young people have much higher expectations of work. They will be involved and participate in work having grown up in schools where they can affect decisions and where authority is questioned and explanations expected. ❜
The Industrial Society

UNEMPLOYMENT

Today many school-leavers are having to face the bitter fact that there is just no work to go to.

The reasons are complex. The world economy is geared to certain crucial commodities: land, for instance, and especially energy sources such as oil. If oil prices go up so much that people cannot afford the goods being made, demand for the goods goes down, demand for oil goes down. People are put out of work so the demand for goods goes down again . . . The result is a vicious spiral leading to massive unemployment.

The economy then has to be 'grown' again, based on different assumptions. People will start up rather different businesses and come up with different ideas, different ways of doing things. If labour has been made too expensive by the unions, the unions will have to think again.

In the meantime, people suffer. Morale, the feeling of self-worth, can be severely knocked if you feel that nobody wants you, if you feel there's no purpose in life . . . So what can we do?

● While waiting for job opportunities to improve, acquire skills or training. You may be able to go on to further education. You may be able to learn to drive, or to cook, or to type, or programme a computer.

● Get work experience, even if temporary or unpaid. Local community schemes may not seem to offer much, but everyone needs work experience. In the future, employers will chose people who have had some experience rather than those who have none. There may be organizations overseas who can use you for short-term service, even if only paying your expenses.

● Use your own initiative. Offering companies a car-wash service (you and some friends) may be your start into your own business . . . After all, many industries which are now household names started in a garage or back bedroom. Perhaps it's *you* who ought

to be creating employment in the future. Think what goods or services people *need* and are prepared to pay for.

● It's not always possible to travel or to look for work elsewhere. If it is, seize the opportunity. Think *where* your skills could be used. Have you relations who will put you up long enough for you to look for work in a more promising area?

● Don't accept the situation. Being out of work is *not* normal. It may take time to do something about it, both as an individual and as a community. God wants each person to make a unique contribution in the world. So keep looking, keep pushing, keep up your determination to fulfil your own particular 'calling' or skill.

HELP FOR THE UNEMPLOYED

In the UK, the government undertakes to give some financial help to people who are out of work; it also has various schemes designed to equip people with skills which may help them in finding a job:

Unemployment benefit Available to anyone who is unemployed, provided that they register as 'available for work' at their local employment office and 'sign on' every fortnight.

Supplementary benefit Additional help if an unemployed person has extra commitments to meet.

Youth Training Scheme A year-long programme for all unemployed 16-year-old and some 17-year-old school-leavers. All-round training must be given, and employers are subsidized to take on extra school-leavers. Under-18s are also eligible for schemes called **Community Project** and **Training Workshops.**

Young Workers' Scheme A school-leaver is taken on *as an employee* by a firm for his/her first job, and the government foots the wage bill for one year.

Community Programme For 18 year olds and over who have been unemployed for at least six months. Work is offered in community work (usually by voluntary/charitable organizations) and the government meets the charity's cost in employing the extra labour.

Community Industry A smallish scheme designed to help deprived/inner city areas and encourage the employment of ex-offenders.

Training Opportunities (TOPS) courses Whole range of training courses (clerical/catering/welding . . .) available to anyone who has been out of full-time education for at least two years. Courses vary in length and those who complete them have a good chance of finding a job.

Development Area Grants Available for firms setting up operations in areas of high unemployment.

GREEDY!

It is vital for people to earn a living wage, and for companies to earn a 'margin' or profit on the goods they sell. Without a profit to finance *next* year's activity, the company will go out of business. But:

● **Employers can be greedy** If the aim is to make money at the expense of workers, this is clearly wrong.

● **Employees can be greedy** If they (or their unions) demand higher wages than a business can afford to pay and still survive, this is greedy (as well as stupid!).

● **Industry can be greedy** If factories ignore the good of the community by polluting water, land, air or environment, this is selfish greed.

● **Governments can be greedy** Taxes can be too high or wages artificially low because of government ambitions or inefficiency.

● **Investors can be greedy** If all that matters is a fat profit, never mind the workers or the product, this is pure greed.

Greed is a result of the basic selfishness of human nature.

Selfishness can also lead to other major problems of work: bad relationships between workers, for instance.

One of the key commands of the Jewish-Christian law and in the teaching of Jesus was 'Love your neighbour as yourself'. Think of the changes in work and industry that would take place if people really *did* this. Jesus offers forgiveness for past sin and power to lead a new life. Do you think this can happen at work, too?

WHAT THE BIBLE SAYS ABOUT WORK

'Then the Lord God placed the man in the Garden of Eden to cultivate it and guard it.' (Genesis 2:15)
God finished his work of creation and gave man creative work to do in looking after the natural environment. Because God worked, there was dignity in work. Work was intended to be a blessing.

★ ★ ★

'Because of what you have done, the ground will be under a curse. You will have to work hard all your life to make it produce enough food for you.' (Genesis 3:17)
It was only after man's relationship with God had been spoiled by disobedience that work became a drudge and a curse.

★ ★ ★

'All of us should eat and drink and enjoy what we have worked for. It is God's gift.' (Ecclesiastes 3:13)
Work and the rewards of it are God's gifts and should be recognized as such. Work brings satisfaction and is an important part of being fully human.

★ ★ ★

'Some people are too lazy to put food in their own mouths.' (Proverbs 26:15)

'. . . keep away from all brothers who are living a lazy life . . . "Whoever refuses to work is not allowed to eat."' (2 Thessalonians 3:6, 10)
Laziness is condemned in the Bible. It criticizes the laziness of people who could work but prefer to avoid it, not the inactivity of the unemployed person who wants work but cannot find it.

★ ★ ★

'Whatever you do, work at it with all your heart, as though you were working for the Lord and not for men.' (Colossians 3:23)
An additional powerful incentive for Christians—work that is done with this attitude will be worthwhile and should be 'a quality job', whether conditions are ideal or not.

★ ★ ★

'He [God] will always make you rich enough to be generous at all times, so that many will thank God for your gifts . . .' (2 Corinthians 9:11)
Those who work are to meet the needs of those who cannot —whether because of illness, bereavement or misfortune. Work is not to be done simply to satisfy our own wants, but as a means of helping others.

homemaking, or teaching, or designing electronic circuits . . . The list is endless. As people develop their skills, exercise their gifts, they will both get job satisfaction and contribute to the community.

● **Making money** Money is what counts in life. You can buy your happiness with a beautiful home, expensive holidays, fast cars . . . So whatever job makes the most money most quickly is the one for me.

● **Community service** The local community cries out for jobs to be done: welfare work, social work, helping the old and the handicapped, health care, nursing, town planning and development, transport . . . Again the list is endless. People can tackle these things as 'just another job'. They may also do them from concern for people or for the community.

● **Career** The important thing in life is to make a career for myself: develop skills and experience, push up the promotion ladder, come out on top . . .

Faith and work

Should your beliefs have anything to do with your work? Many people would say not. What you believe is private: it shouldn't affect the everyday world of work.

But what you believe determines how you behave. Here are some examples of the way different faiths have affected people's attitudes to work:

● **Fatalism** If you think that nothing you can do will make any difference to life, it's all predetermined by God or the stars, you won't bother to try to change it. Is it a good thing to say 'It's the will of Allah, the will of God' and sit back and do nothing?

● **Domination** In communities dominated by feudal ideas of master and servant, or hierarchy, or the rule of wealthy land-owners, it's easy for people to be exploited. The poor are kept poor, and the strong can easily take advantage of the weak. Working conditions may be bad—dirty, too cold or too hot, dark, dangerous or noisy. In Hindu countries, the 'caste' system means that some people are 'the lowest of the low', fit only for the most menial jobs.

● **Christianity** The Bible teaches that man has been made to work: but that since sin came into the world, work is difficult, it's a toil and struggle. Christianity also teaches concern for others; development of the world and its resources; working to please God and help your fellow-men. Areas of Europe and America most influenced by this (especially Protestant) work ethic have developed rapidly.

Discussion topics

1 What would your ideal job be and why?

2 How would you define 'work'?

3 'All employment is work, but not all work is employment.' Do you agree? Would you do voluntary work if you were unemployed?

4 Is any job better than none?

5 Do you think that 'anyone can get a job if they really want one'?

6 Do you think that trades unions have too much or too little power?

7 Do you believe in 'working to live' or 'living to work'?

8 Should schools give as much time to preparing school-leavers for possible unemployment as they do to careers advice?

9 Should the government introduce tariff barriers so that cheap foreign goods cannot be imported and compete with home-produced items?

10 What do you think of the idea of job-sharing—two people working part-time on the same job rather than one having a full-time job and one being on the dole? What if *you* were asked to share *your* job in this way?

WHAT THE BIBLE SAYS

To employers
'"You have six days in which to do your work . . ."' (Exodus 20:9)

'The Sabbath [rest day] was made for the good of man; man was not made for the Sabbath.' (Mark 2:27)
Do not demand unreasonably long hours—there must be time off from work for rest and relaxation.

★   ★   ★

'"Do not take advantage of anyone or rob him. Do not hold back the wages of someone you have hired, not even for one night."' (Leviticus 19:13)

'A worker should be given his pay.' (Luke 10:7)
Pay a fair wage as reward for a worker's time and effort. He is not a 'work machine' to be bought, sold, exploited or treated inhumanely.

★   ★   ★

'Masters [employers], be fair and just in the way you treat your slaves. Remember that you too have a Master in heaven.' (Colossians 4:1)
Treat your workforce fairly.

To employees
'Slaves [employees], obey your human masters [employers] with fear and trembling; and do it with a sincere heart, as though you were serving Christ. Do this not only when they are watching you, because you want to gain their approval . . . Do your work . . . cheerfully, as though you served the Lord, and not merely men.' (Ephesians 6:5–7)
'If a job's worth doing, it's worth doing well'—and not just when the boss is looking either! Christians have the added incentive of wanting to please God by working well.

To both
'The Lord wants weights and measures to be honest and every sale to be fair.' (Proverbs 16:11)
Make sure you are not cheating anyone of money, time or a good name. Make all transactions honest and 'above board'.

★   ★   ★

'Does a person gain anything if he wins the whole world but loses his life? Of course not!' (Mark 8:36)
Don't make the love of money and material things your prime motivation for work. If it is, it can lead to exploitation, greed and dubious business practices.

PART 3
INTERNATIONAL ISSUES

WHY DOESN'T GOD STOP THE FIGHTING?

Why should I worry about the starving millions?

UNIT 18

WAR

We are used to the news media bringing us reports of conflicts around the world—rebellions, terrorism, uprisings, civil disturbances and riots, states of emergency and army takeovers.

The costliest and most destructive kind of conflict is war. To distinguish war from other kinds of conflict, it has been defined as 'an outbreak of violence which involves the use of regular armed forces by at least one side, with the use of weapons, for at least one hour'. On this basis, there have been over 100 wars since the Second World War ended in 1945.

Causes

A particular war may have an 'immediate cause' or flashpoint situation which triggers off the conflict. For example, the Americans joined in the Second World War in 1941 because the Japanese attacked their navy in Pearl Harbour. The 1948 war between Israel and her Arab neighbours was sparked off by Israel's declaration of independence. The UK entered the war against Germany in 1914 because a treaty had been signed to help Belgium in the event of invasion.

Underlying the immediate causes, however, are a number of deeper reasons for war, sometimes described as 'intermediate causes' (see Unit 11, Crime). The difference in politics between the Western nations and

those of the communist bloc have been beneath the surface in wars which have taken place in Korea and Vietnam. Intense Turkish and Greek nationalism has been involved in Cyprus, and strong nationalistic and religious feelings have affected the conflict between Iran and Iraq. Injustice and oppression have been the deeper causes behind wars in Indonesia and Uganda.

Perhaps injustice lies deeper than other intermediate causes. *Why* do people want wealth and land which belong to others? *Why* do people oppress others and treat them unjustly? *Why* are some people cruel and aggressive? Christians would say that the reason lies in human nature, which is basically greedy, evil and selfish, and that all wars can be traced back to these characteristics at source. Christians refer to this fundamental problem as 'sin'.

Effects

Because warfare is conflict on a large scale, involving deadly weapons, (usually) thousands of people over a considerable period of time, it has devastating and far-reaching effects.

● **Death** This is the most obvious effect of war—but it has *quantitative* and *qualitative* aspects. It has been calculated that 59 million people were killed in wars between 1820 and 1945—6 million of these were Jews who were exterminated in the concentration camps of central Europe during the Second World War. The first atomic bomb, dropped on Hiroshima in Japan in

Cemeteries from the First and Second World Wars are a sobering sight. Each grave represents heartache and grief in some home or family. Fathers, husbands and sons were killed, often leaving families without a bread-winner.

1945, destroyed 60,000 people. War claims the lives of many innocent victims as well as those of the fighting troops.

Society is always the poorer after a war, because the fittest men often give their lives during wartime. War could be seen as the most senseless waste of talent ever devised.

● **Injury** Injuries to body and mind caused by war leave people scarred for life—either through a physical

---

PERHAPS . . .
To R. A. L.

Perhaps some day the sun will
 shine again,
And I shall see that still the skies
 are blue,
And feel once more I do not live
 in vain,
Although bereft of You.

Perhaps the golden meadows at
 my feet
Will make the sunny hours of
 spring seem gay,
And I shall find the white May-
 blossoms sweet,
Though You have passed away.

Perhaps the summer woods will
 shimmer bright,
And crimson roses once again be
 fair,
And autumn harvest fields a rich
 delight,
Although You are not there.

But though kind Time may
 many joys renew,
There is one greatest joy I shall
 not know
Again, because my heart for loss
 of You
Was broken, long ago.

From *Verses of a V.A.D.*, by Vera Brittain, 1916; quoted in *Testament of Youth*. Her fiancé was killed in action in France.

---

disability or the lingering after-effects of mental and emotional suffering.

● **Refugees** People in a battle zone often decide to leave their homes, livelihoods and virtually all their personal belongings behind and flee from the opposing armies. They may choose to go across the border to a

neighbouring (peaceful) country, in the hope of finding help and support. Often the receiving country has no spare housing, work or surplus food to give to the refugees—they are homeless and stateless. Sometimes there is no hope of a return home, and the refugee camps may become

breeding grounds of hopelessness and bitterness.

● **Destruction** War has always left a trail of destruction in its wake, but the sheer scale of modern warfare means that the potential threat to the whole planet is far greater. Nuclear weapons already available could kill

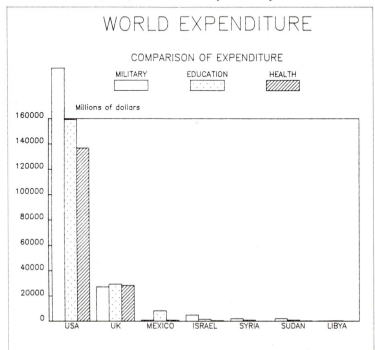

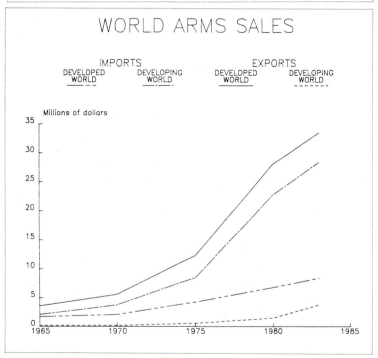

the entire world population several times over. Chemical and biological (germ) warfare can kill or disable people; it also destroys food supplies and changes and upsets the balance of nature as vegetation is destroyed and water is poisoned. Not only does a nuclear bomb devastate large areas, but the radio-active cloud which follows the explosion drifts with the air currents, and the 'fall-out' destroys living things in its path.

● **Cost** Looked at just in financial terms, war is an incredible waste of resources. The cost of pensions and support payments when there is death or permanent injury, and of rebuilding cities or reclaiming land after a war, is almost too great to be imagined. Even when a war does not actually occur, the cost of defence (or preparing for war) is enormous. In 1979–80, the total amount spent on defence by the British government was £5,243 million—on weapons, payment of the armed forces,

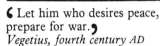

❬ Let him who desires peace, prepare for war.❭
Vegetius, fourth century AD

maintenance of equipment, research and development, etc. This is a large proportion of total government spending. If this kind of money is spent on defence, it is clear that it cannot be spent on the provision of roads, new housing, education and social services.

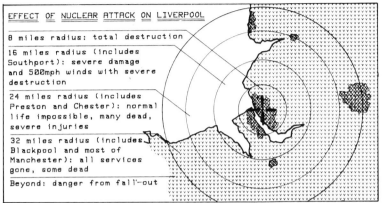

EFFECT OF NUCLEAR ATTACK ON LIVERPOOL

8 miles radius: total destruction

16 miles radius (includes Southport): severe damage and 500mph winds with severe destruction

24 miles radius (includes Preston and Chester): normal life impossible, many dead, severe injuries

32 miles radius (includes Blackpool and most of Manchester): all services gone, some dead

Beyond: danger from fall'-out

THE INTERNATIONAL RED CROSS

When a war breaks out, or a disaster strikes, we are used to hearing that Red Cross workers are on the scene.

The Red Cross began in Switzerland through the work of one man—Henri Dunant. Dunant was born into a wealthy Geneva family in 1828. His Christian concern led him to spend all his spare time helping the poor—using most of his savings to buy medicine, food and clothing.

In 1859, Dunant travelled to northern Italy to try to meet the Emperor Napoleon personally and request permission to extend the farm he had established in Algeria (French territory). In Italy, he witnessed one of the worst battles of the Franco-Austrian war, at Solferino, and the experience changed his life.

In the twelve-hour battle, 40,000 men were killed or wounded. Dunant tried to organize help for the wounded in the nearby town of Castiglione, but it was extremely difficult. There was no provision of food or water, so that men who could not move died of hunger and thirst. Only two doctors were available. There were no beds, no medicines, no bandages and nobody to care for the wounded and dying. Dunant managed as best he could, caring for Austrian and French soldiers alike. He persuaded Napoleon to release captured doctors so that they could help the wounded.

After the battle, the horror of the situation stayed with him. He believed that the wounded in battle had a right to help, whatever their nationality. His book, *A Memory of Solferino*, published in 1862, suggested that trained helpers should be brought together in peace-time, organized internationally, and that they should be ready to help the wounded in war anywhere and at any time.

One of the people who read the book was Gustave Moynier, then president of the Geneva Welfare Society. He called an international meeting to discuss the ideas put forward by Dunant. Dunant himself wrote to many governments to try to persuade them to send a representative. The meeting was held in 1863 and it was agreed that the representatives would return a year later with the reactions of their governments. On their return in 1864, they signed a document known as 'The Geneva Convention'.

It was agreed by the governments which signed that:
● Every wounded soldier would be cared for.
● Those who cared for the wounded would receive protection.
● The sign these helpers would use to identify themselves would be the reverse of the Geneva flag.

As the movement grew, the international committee became the International Red Cross. The committee has twenty-five members, all Swiss, because Switzerland has always remained neutral in war. There are at present 126 Red Cross-affiliated societies throughout the world. The original Geneva Convention has been changed since 1864 to meet the needs of modern warfare, and clauses about victims of war at sea, and the treatment of prisoners of war have been added. Its signatories agree to observe the rules of behaviour in war that the convention lays down.

One national Red Cross Society may be formed in each country which is a signatory. Any person may become a member, no matter what their colour, race or religion. In the UK, the society's work is carried out by county branches, each of which is an independent charity. There are 139,000 young and adult members who give their time unpaid. Part of their work is fund-raising, but most of it is helping people who need their services. Food and clothing parcels are sent to those in need, exchanges of sick prisoners are arranged, complaints are made to governments when the terms of the Geneva Convention are not kept, missing persons are traced in wartime. Since 1919, the Red Cross has also provided relief in the case of disasters other than warfare.

A Christian perspective

You may have often wanted to ask how Christians can believe in a God of love, when he allows wars to take place? If he cares about the world (as Christians say), why doesn't he step in and stop all the madness and bloodshed? And how come Christians—who are supposed to be 'peacemakers'—sometimes go to war along with everyone else?

Christians believe that God created everyone with free-will—that is, the freedom and ability in any given situation to choose between right and wrong. Often the motive governing our choice is self-interest: 'What do *I* want?' 'What will suit *me* best?'

'What's in it for *me*?'

Christians also believe that wars are started because of self-interest on a national (or global) scale: '*My* country, right or wrong', 'That disputed territory really belongs to *us*'.

So, if God were to stop all wars, he would have to take away our freedom. In other words, we would need to become mindless robots—a solution that would not fit with the Christian God whose love for mankind means that he gives us the dignity of being free to choose (rather like parents do with their children). We have to learn then to live with the consequences of our decisions.

The tragedy is that humankind has chosen to live for self, not for God. Our freedom of action has led to a new bondage: to sin, selfishness, suffering, death. Until freed by Jesus Christ, we have a built-in bias to wrong-doing.

Definition

What is war, my lord?
War is empire.

What is war, general?
War is manhood.

What is war, teacher?
War is inevitable.

What is war, preacher?
War is unfortunate.

What is war, fellow?
War is escape.

What is war, kind employer?
War is profit.

Sister, what is war?
War is a telegram.

Brother, what is war?
War is my powerlessness.

Father, what is war?
War is my trembling hand.

Mother, what is war?
War is undiscovered graves.

L. Collinson

WHAT THE BIBLE SAYS ABOUT WAR

'You are doomed! You make unjust laws that oppress my people. That is how you prevent the poor from having their rights and from getting justice . . . What will you do when God punishes you? What will you do when he brings disaster on you from a distant country? . . . You will be killed in battle or dragged off as prisoners.' (Isaiah 10:1–4)

The Old Testament has many accounts of wars and fighting— some of them pretty bloodthirsty! They seem to teach that God sometimes uses warfare as a way of punishing evil and cruel nations, and of putting an end to injustice and oppression.

★ ★ ★

'He [Jesus] will settle disputes among great nations. They will hammer their swords into ploughs and their spears into pruning-knives. Nations will never again go to war, never prepare for battle again.' (Isaiah 2:4)

'The Lord says, "I will remove the war-chariots from Israel and take the horses from Jerusalem; the bows used in battle will be destroyed. Your king will make peace among the nations; he will rule from sea to sea."' (Zechariah 9:10)

But God also hates war and the suffering it brings. The Old Testament prophets looked forward to the coming of the Messiah, who would put an end to all wars and usher in a kingdom of peace. Christians believe this will happen when world history ends at the second coming of Jesus Christ to earth.

★ ★ ★

'"You are going to hear the noise of battles close by and the news of battles far away; but do not be troubled. Such things must happen . . . Countries will fight each other, kingdoms will attack one another."' (Matthew 24:6–7)

Jesus told his followers not to be surprised at the outbreak of wars all over the world.

★ ★ ★

'"Put your sword back in its place," Jesus said . . . "All who take the sword will die by the sword."' (Matthew 26:52)

Jesus' example was one of non-violence. His words apply to what is happening in the modern world—the vicious circle of war breeding war.

★ ★ ★

'Where do all the fights and quarrels among you come from? They come from your desires for pleasure, which are constantly fighting within you. You want things, but you cannot have them, so you are ready to kill; you strongly desire things, but you cannot get them, so you quarrel and fight.' (James 4:1–2)

The Bible gets to the root cause of all wars—it is ultimately man's greed and selfishness which trigger off disputes and conflicts.

★ ★ ★

'What [the Lord] requires of us is this: to do what is just, to show constant love, and to live in humble fellowship with our God.' (Micah 6:8)

The key factors for Christians are justice and love. According to these principles, some Christians would fight against an evil aggressor (e.g. Hitler), while others would say that no action in war can be truly loving and therefore refuse to take up arms.

Christians find themselves in a difficult position. They are citizens of both worlds—old and new. Is it right to fight or not? Nowhere in the Bible does it say that followers of Jesus are not to go to war. It is clear that violence is not to take place at a personal level: Christians are commanded to love their neighbours, try to settle quarrels quickly and not to take revenge but to live in peace and leave judgement to God. The commandment not to kill applies to committing murder. Does it also mean not killing judicially or in the cause of right and freedom? If we 'love our enemies', as Jesus taught in the Sermon on the Mount, there seems to be no room for warfare. But what about when we are acting as citizens of our country?

Christians therefore have to decide whether or not the commands to live in peace at a personal level also apply to living in peace on a national and international level. This has resulted in Christians adopting different approaches, which are also shared by people who do not hold Christian beliefs.

Pietism

Christian pietists have believed that they should opt out of politics, courts, trades unions and military service—in fact, anything to do with the workings of the state. The reason behind this is that Jesus distinguished between his 'spiritual kingdom' and earthly, political kingdoms. He said that his followers would be hated because they 'do not belong to the world, just as I do not belong to the world'. Pietists point out that Christians are called to fight a spiritual battle against evil, not a physical battle with weapons and armies.

Christians who have taken this point of view often choose to be 'conscientious objectors' if they are called up for military service. This is not an easy way out—in Britain at the time of the First World War it meant imprisonment as well as ridicule and accusations of treachery and cowardice.

The just war

The New Testament makes it clear that Christians are expected to obey the government (see Unit 13, Authority). Since it is part of a government's responsibility to carry out 'God's punishment on those who do evil', the Christian has to support his rulers if they feel that policing or war are necessary. Christians, therefore, should be prepared to fight for their country, but insist that it must be a 'just war'—that the war must be justified, and must be conducted properly.

In the thirteenth century, Thomas Aquinas said that a war is 'just':
● if it is started by the **proper authority** of the sovereign (i.e. it could not be waged by private citizens);
● if there is **sufficient cause** (self-defence, to right wrongs, to restore what has been taken unjustly);
● if it is waged with **good intention** (with the aim of securing common good, bringing about peace and restoring good relations with the enemy);
● if **all three conditions are fulfilled together.**

In the sixteenth century, the Dutchman Grotius added two further rules of conduct about just warfare:
● **discrimination:** non-combatants should be protected from attack;
● **proportion:** methods used should be restricted to those which will secure achievement of the aim(s).

THE CHURCH AND THE BOMB

No one can afford to ignore the issues raised by the nuclear debate—least of all the Christian church. There are important religious and moral, as well as military and political, considerations.

As a major contribution to this debate, a Working Party of the Church of England's Board for Social Responsibility looked at the whole area of nuclear weapons and Christian conscience. Their report, *The Church and the Bomb*, was published in October 1982, and combined an analysis of the technical issues, an investigation of the underlying moral questions and detailed recommendations concerning NATO and the British nuclear deterrent.

The report said that for Britain to opt for unilateral disarmament would be 'a positive and courageous stand'. Leaving the nuclear arms race would free up resources 'to serve other causes on which the future of humanity also depends'. Nuclear weapons could not be treated in isolation from the whole problem of war; nuclear disarmament was only the first and most urgent task in the process of ridding the world of any kind of war. To persist in pinning hopes on nuclear weapons was to gamble with the lives and well-being of the innocent and unborn, and no one had the right to do that. The Working Party firmly believed that *'the cause of right cannot be upheld by fighting a nuclear war'*.

The Working Party's report was debated by the General Synod of the Church of England in February 1983 and many different views were expressed. The option of unilateral disarmament was rejected, and the following motion eventually agreed:
'That this Synod recognizing,
(a) the urgency of the task of making and preserving peace;
(b) the extreme seriousness of the threat made to the world by contemporary nuclear weapons and the dangers in the present situation, and
(c) that it is not the task of the Church to determine defence strategy but rather to give a moral lead to the nation;
(1) affirms that it is the duty of HM Government and her allies to maintain adequate forces to guard against nuclear blackmail and to deter nuclear and non-nuclear aggressors;
(2) asserts that the tactics and strategies of this country and her NATO allies should be seen to be unmistakably defensive in respect of the countries of the Warsaw Pact;
(3) judges that even a small-scale first use of nuclear weapons could never be morally justified in view of the high risk that this would lead to full-scale nuclear warfare;
(4) believes that there is a moral obligation on all countries (including the members of NATO) publicly to forswear the first use of nuclear weapons in any form;
(5) bearing in mind that many in Europe live in fear of nuclear catastrophe and that nuclear parity is not essential to deterrence, calls on HM Government to take immediate steps in conjunction with her allies to further the principles embodied in this motion so as to reduce progressively NATO's dependence on nuclear weapons and to decrease nuclear arsenals throughout the world.'

These are still regarded as moral principles in warfare, but modern weapons are making them increasingly difficult to apply. In fact, many argue today that nuclear weapons make a 'just war' impossible, because they cannot discriminate between combatants and non-combatants. This is a new situation, they argue; nuclear weapons are immoral and the Christian must oppose them.

Pacifism

A pacifist is a person who is opposed to war and the use of force, and who believes that the abolition of war is both desirable and possible. However, instead of completely opting out, he tries to use non-violent means of protesting against war and of promoting peace. Christian pacifists find support in the apostle Paul's instruction to 'overcome evil with good'. This positive approach is very important —peace is not just the absence of war and conflict; it involves harmony,

In war, children are often the innocent victims of a situation they do not understand. Refugees from the horrors of war may find themselves in camps or shanty towns, depending on emergency relief from the rich nations until (hopefully) they can return home or be sent to a third country.

> ❮ Violence is the policy of barbarians; non-violence is the policy of men. ❯
> *Mahatma Gandhi*

equality and justice (all the concepts in the Israeli greeting, *shalom*, which we translate 'peace').

Quakers are a Christian group who are well known for their stand on pacifism. They made two submissions outlining their views to the United Nations Assembly when disarmament was being considered:
● Armaments are not a means of security, but a threat to peace. They are a tragic waste of human and material resources.
● Every human being is important in the sight of God. Therefore we must not risk turning the world into an atomic cinder; we must have peaceful ways of settling disputes.
● Security should be based on the solving of world problems such as famine, water supply, disease and pollution.

Increasing numbers of Christians are adopting the position of non-violent protest. They point out that

Jesus always stood with the oppressed, and confronted those who misused their wealth and influence. He refused to use force himself and would not identify himself with the Zealots, who were the armed terrorists of his day. His earliest followers spoke out against the Jewish authorities, but they did not try to bring the government down. When the apostle Paul wrote to Christians at Ephesus, he said that the Christian has the job of showing the world what God wants to do for it—to deal with both the immediate and intermediate causes of war by offering a new life in Jesus which will deal with the underlying problems of human greed and selfishness. When a person's relationship with God is put right in this way, his attitudes and reactions to, and relationships with, his fellow human beings will be transformed too.

Assignments and discussion topics

1 Since 1948, wars have been fought in the following countries: Cuba, Chile, Northern Ireland, Hungary, Cyprus, Israel, Suez, Lebanon, Zaïre (Congo), Nigeria, Uganda, Zimbabwe (Rhodesia), Angola, Afghanistan, Ethiopia, Tibet, Kashmir, Bangladesh, Vietnam, Iraq, Kampuchea (Cambodia), Indonesia and Korea. Choose any six of these and try to find out for each:
● what triggered it off;
● what it was about;
● who was fighting whom;
● how long it lasted;
● what the outcome was.

2 The Jewish *Talmud* says, 'If a person intends to kill you, be first to kill him.' The Muslim *Qur'an* says, 'Fight in the way of Allah with those who fight you, but do not begin hostilities.' Is a defensive war therefore OK?

3 Is it good or bad to be reminded of 'what happened in the war'? Should we just 'forgive and forget'?

4 When 40 per cent of the world's population is on the brink of starvation, is it morally right to spend such vast sums on ways of destroying other people or on defence projects such as the American Strategic Defence Initiative (Star Wars Project)?

5 'If faced with the choice of living without many of the things that give life value and make it worthwhile, or to die to preserve those things, it is better to die.' What things give life value and make it worthwhile for you? Do you agree with the quote?

6 Imagine yourself as a war refugee. What would your feelings be?

7 Which of the three Christian approaches to war do you agree with and why?

8 The most recent war that Britain has been involved in was the Falklands conflict in 1982. What were your feelings about that? Did it fit any or all of the conditions for a 'just war'?

9 Some people oppose 'Peace Studies' in school because they believe it is a one-sided way of looking at war and the need for defence. How could Peace Studies be done so as to avoid indoctrination into any particular viewpoint?

UNIT 19

POVERTY

'Poor' means different things to different people. When a rich man's family complains that death duties on his country estate will make them 'poor', their poverty still means that they have more wealth than an unemployed labourer in the inner city could ever dream about. When a person in the UK says that he is 'poor' because he is out of work and cannot afford to go on holiday or continue the payments on the car, his wealth is still so great that an African peasant could not imagine it. There are obviously different degrees of poverty.

Some people have tried to describe what poverty *does*, rather than what it *is*. When David Sheppard left county cricket and worked in the Mayflower Christian Community Centre in the East End of London, he came to believe that poverty meant the same thing as powerlessness. If a person is poor, he has no power to influence others, or to improve his situation.

The 'Third World'

The low-income, hungry nations of the world form a group which can be easily identified (see map: 'The great divide: rich and poor'). They are not part of the Western world or the oil-producing nations; they do not include most of the countries with communist governments where there is a centrally-planned economy. The low-income group of countries is frequently referred to as the 'Third World'.

This term was first used by French journalists. In the period prior to the French Revolution in 1789 there were two groups of privileged people in French society: the nobility and the higher ranks of the clergy. The remainder, or underprivileged group, was called the 'tiers état' (third estate, or third world). In the mid-

INDICATORS OF POVERTY

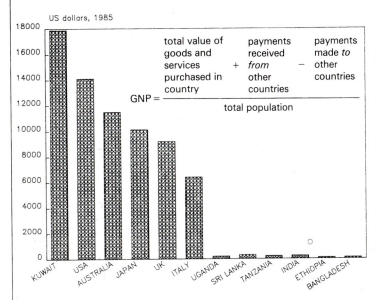

GROSS NATIONAL PRODUCT
PER YEAR PER HEAD OF POPULATION

US dollars, 1985

$$GNP = \frac{\text{total value of goods and services purchased in country} + \text{payments received from other countries} - \text{payments made to other countries}}{\text{total population}}$$

The GNP figure is calculated *per year per head of population* – a high figure indicates a wealthy country and a low figure indicates a poor country. The World Bank, which provides financial and technical assistance to help in the development of poor member states, classifies 'low income countries' as those having a GNP below $250. It is estimated that 800 million people in the world are living in absolute poverty.

● **Calorie intake** Calories (in the dietary sense) are units of energy value in food and supply the energy needed for the body to function well. Average calorie intakes provide another measure of relative poverty.

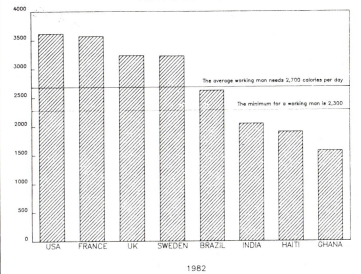

CALORIE INTAKE
PER PERSON PER DAY

The average working man needs 2,700 calories per day

The minimum for a working man is 2,300

1982

THE GREAT DIVIDE: RICH AND POOR

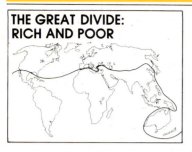

twentieth century, the term was applied to the poor nations of the world, because the writers felt that their position was very similar to that of most French people before the revolution.

The Third World nations are sometimes also called the 'developing nations', and Western countries 'developed nations'. A developed nation is one which has been able to use industry to create wealth so that its people enjoy a large income (and high GNP) each year. Developing nations are those which are trying to raise their GNP year by year, but find it difficult to improve their underprivileged position for a number of reasons:

● **Lack of money** The basic problem is the lack of paid employment. At an individual level, people are too poor to provide basic necessities for themselves such as food, clothing and a roof over their heads. At a national level, the government cannot afford to provide adequate social services, health care, a safe water supply, education and transport facilities. The combined effect of these deficiencies is to make the life expectancy of people in Third World countries much lower than in the rest of the world.

LIFE EXPECTANCY IN 1983

	Male	Female
USA	67	72
UK	68	71
USSR	65	65
INDIA	46	56
CHAD	39	42
GUINEA	34	37

The lack of money is a problem in other ways too. In many poor countries, much perfectly good food is destroyed by pests. It is estimated that 50 per cent of India's agricultural produce is lost through insects, rodents and mildew; Latin

America loses about 30 per cent. Locusts in one swarm can eat 100,000 tons of green plants in one day. Only goats and poultry can live in 6 million square miles (all within the Third World) infested by the tsetse fly, which spreads a disease fatal to cattle. Crops can be saved by building good storage facilities and by using pesticides, but this cannot be done if there is no money.

● **Hunger and malnutrition**
When there is not enough money for food, two different problems arise. If there is insufficient food *of any kind*, children die from a disease known as marasmus. The child's body becomes skinny and wasted, his skin becomes shrivelled and his eyes large and staring. Vomiting and diarrhoea reduce the level of body fluids and death is the result.

Insufficient food *of the right kind* causes other diseases. Kwashiorkor is due to lack of protein, normally after the mother has stopped breast-feeding her baby. The child stops growing, loses weight, gets a distended stomach, loses hair, develops diarrhoea and begins to look prematurely old. If the child survives, he becomes a weak and lethargic adult with no energy or desire to work.

In some countries, religious taboos on eating certain foods (for example, the cow is sacred to the Hindu and Muslims will not eat pork) mean that much potential protein goes to waste.

● **Population explosion** The staggering population growth in developing countries means that available wealth and resources have to be 'spread thinly'. Over 1 million people are added to the population of the world every five days, and it will increase in the 1980s and 1990s by close to 2 billion; 90 per cent of the increase will take place in the Third World. Rapid growth over a long time has produced (and will continue to do so) a very young age structure in developing countries; the number of new families will grow so fast that

❛ Give a man a fish and you feed him for a day; teach him to fish and you feed him for life. ❜

even if each couple starting from today had only two children, their population would increase by almost one-third.

● **Lack of resources** Less than one-third of the world's land surface can be cultivated for crops. The 11,000 million acres which *can* be

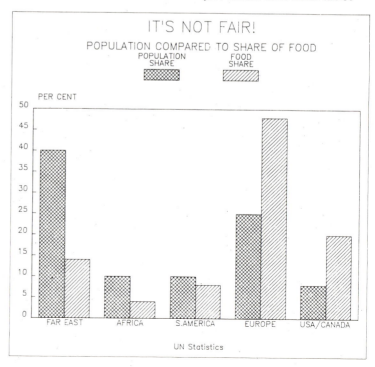

IT'S NOT FAIR!
POPULATION COMPARED TO SHARE OF FOOD

UN Statistics

used are not in the same place as the bulk of the world's population—the resources are missing where there is the greatest need for them. A simple comparison between India and Canada shows the kind of difference:

	India & SE Asia	Canada
% world's population	45	6
% world's food grown	25	22
% land cultivated	95	17

There are also historical reasons for the lack of resources in developing countries. Most of them were at one time colonies of the great powers (mainly Britain and Spain). When a colonial government was set up, the economy of the country was geared to European needs. Instead of growing a variety of crops, countries were turned over to the production of the one crop which could be grown most successfully—coffee, tea, cocoa, rice—whatever that particular country was best suited to. Other resources were ignored.

As former colonies have gained their independence, they have often found that their economies are dangerously dependent on only one basic resource. If disease or a natural disaster causes crop failure, or if the world price for that commodity drops, the country's economy is in serious trouble.

In some cases, native industry in countries conquered by colonists was destroyed. India had a thriving cotton and textile industry before colonization by the British. But as the mills of Lancashire developed, cotton exports to Britain from India fell by 1,300 per cent between 1815 and 1832, while British exports to India rose by 1,600 per cent over the same period.

● **Cycles of depression** If someone finds that they cannot sleep because they are worried, they begin to feel over-strained and unwell. Worry about the strain and illness makes sleep even less likely and the problem gets worse. This may go on until the person reaches a state of collapse, or their doctor prescribes some sleeping tablets to induce sleep and reverse the cycle.

THE GREAT DIVIDE: RICH AND POOR DIETS

A balanced diet is one containing an adequate supply of protein, fat, carbohydrate, vitamins and fibre. A typical Third World diet is rich in carbohydrates and fibre, but lacks adequate protein and vitamins. A comparison of the diets eaten each day in the UK, India and South America demonstrates the differences between rich and poor diets:

Food supplies in ounces per day per person in:

	UK	India	Ecuador
Cereals	7.32	12.20	6.32
Potatoes	9.67	1.38	11.18
Sugar	4.80	1.76	3.42
Vegetables	5.96	0.08	4.34
Meat	7.09	0.14	2.08
Eggs	1.55	0.04	0.18
Fish	0.92	0.11	0.28
Milk	20.19	3.88	3.53
Fats/oils	2.19	0.32	0.46

The shortage of protein in Third World diets stunts growth, and vitamin deficiencies can cause serious illnesses:
Vitamin A deficiency: blindness
Vitamin B deficiency: paralysis, heart failure, nervous disorders, skin disease, loss of body fluids, mental subnormality
Vitamin D deficiency: bone deformities

THE GREAT DIVIDE: RICH AND POOR SPENDING PATTERNS

● **Annual spending in the UK**
Official development assistance

1980 — 1854 million
1981 — 2192 million
1982 — 1800 million
1983 — 1605 million
1984 — 1432 million

Slimming aids	45 million
Cat food	75 million
Sweets	750 million
Alcohol	2180 million
Tobacco	2520 million
Total	5570 million

Assuming a UK population of around 56 million, the average amount spent on cats, remedial medicine for overeating, plus food and drink which does positive harm is about $99 per person per year.

● Compare this with the GNP of five developing countries (the annual amount spent by each person on *everything* (food, clothing, shelter . . .):

Mali	$160
Burma	$180
Zaire	$170
Malawi	$210
India	$260

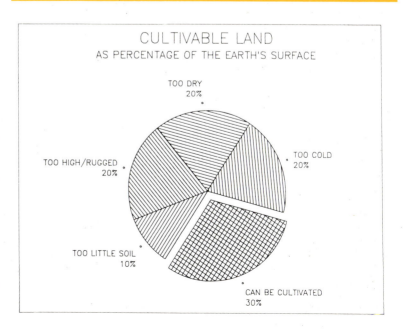

CULTIVABLE LAND
AS PERCENTAGE OF THE EARTH'S SURFACE

TOO DRY 20%
TOO COLD 20%
TOO HIGH/RUGGED 20%
TOO LITTLE SOIL 10%
CAN BE CULTIVATED 30%

The same kind of thing can happen in economic terms, too. Most farmers in the Third World are 'subsistence farmers'—they produce just enough for their family's own needs. However, there may occasionally be some surplus food (in a good year) and the money obtained from selling this may enable the farmer to buy extra grain, some tools or other 'extras' for his family.

But—if he cannot produce enough food to feed his family (perhaps because of drought, floods or attacks by pests), they suffer malnutrition and some may become ill and die. The effects of disease, malnutrition and the smaller family unit make it impossible for any more food to be grown. There is then even less to live on. Unless an outsider injects money, better tools or better seed into this cycle, it will get steadily worse. This situation is sadly very common in the Third World.

● **Injustice and greed in the rich world** The USA has 10 per cent of the world's population but consumes 40 per cent of its resources (food, fuel, minerals, etc). The other rich nations—making up 20 per cent of

world population—use a further 30 per cent of the world's resources. The remaining 30 per cent of resources have to be shared between 70 per cent of the world's people. It has been estimated that the average American draws on resources that would support fifty Indians! By any standards, this is an unequal and unfair distribution of the world's wealth, but it seems that the rich nations of the world are determined to improve their own standard of

---

❛ Enough for each man's need, not each man's greed. ❜

---

living even if it is at the expense of the Third World countries.

One of the reasons why the West consumes so much of the world's *food* resources, for instance, is because grain is used to fatten animals for meat. When this happens, there is a great reduction in the actual food value. Ten per cent of the grain fed to cattle in the West in 1974 would have met the need for grain in the whole of Asia. The USA recently imported 500,000 tons of

HELP FOR THE THIRD WORLD
There are a number of organizations (mostly charities) which are involved in trying to help Third World countries:
● **Oxfam** (274 Banbury Road, Oxford OX2 7DZ)
Started in 1942 as 'Oxford Committee for Famine Relief', helping war refugees in Europe. Became known as Oxfam in 1950, its aim being 'to relieve suffering arising out of war or any other cause in any part of the world'.
● **Christian Aid** (POB 1, London SW9 8BH)
Part of the British Council of Churches, which links together most Christian denominations in the UK. Grants are made to any groups in need: to improve agriculture, provide clean water, medical training, emergency relief and community development programmes.
● **War on Want** (467 Caledonian Road, London N7 9BE)
'Association for World Peace' formed in 1951 and produced a statement

fish meal for cattle-feed—the fish meal would have provided enough protein for 15 million people for a year. Because meat-eating has become fashionable in the Western

---

TRADE, NOT AID

The rich countries of the world do give aid (often 'with strings attached') to the Third World, but the poorer countries are more interested in a 'leg-up' rather than a 'hand-out'—that is, being given the chance to develop their own industries to give them long-term security, rather than constantly having to depend on foreign charity. It is in the area of trading regulations that the Third World countries have found themselves at a great disadvantage, and have used the United Nations Conference on Trade and Development (UNCTAD)—held every four years—as a way of seeking help from the rich nations over trade. They have asked that:
● **Prices of raw materials be index-linked to the price of manufactured goods** In 1960, three tons of bananas or 165 bags of coffee 'bought' one tractor; in 1970, it cost the equivalent of eleven tons of bananas, or 316 bags of coffee. In 1970, ten pounds of Indian tea would buy 2.6 bushels of wheat, but by 1974, the same amount

would buy only 1.7 bushels. This means that the only hope for the poor countries is to have the two sets of prices (for exported raw materials and for imported manufactured goods) linked together.
● **Tariffs and quotas be relaxed** Western countries often add a tax to imported goods from the poor countries: 2 per cent on raw materials, 5 per cent on unfinished goods, 10 per cent on finished goods, saying that the removal of tariffs and quotas would put their own workers out of jobs. Only 2 per cent of the UK's imports actually comes from Third World countries, and the World Bank has suggested that if trade barriers were removed, the money earned by poorer countries as a result would then be used to purchase more goods from the rich countries.
● **A common fund be set up to stabilize prices** Zambia's main export is copper: the world copper price per ton in three successive years was £400, £1,400 and £550. Tanzania exports sisal: the world sisal price dropped from £148 to £70 per ton in five years. When this happens to a country's

major export, it makes nonsense of any economic planning and can lead a poor country to ruination. The suggestion was therefore made that the rich countries should set up a fund to stockpile resources when there was a surplus, and sell them at a set price when they were scarce.
● **Multinational companies be asked to fulfil responsibilities to those out of whom their profits are made** Multinational companies such as Coca-Cola, Shell, Ford, Unilever and Mitsubishi try to control every part of the process of buying and selling. They set up companies to produce crops or extract minerals, to transport them, to process or manufacture them, to market the product, and still others to cover the insurance, packaging and advertising. In this way, the parent company tries to ensure the highest possible profit. Such companies can do a great deal to help poorer countries by investment, and the hope was that their responsibilities could be made clear to them.

called 'War on Want' in 1952. Organization adopted this as its name. Seeks to make people aware of situations which cause suffering and poverty, and sends money to local groups to support them in their efforts for improvement.

● **World Development Movement** (Bedford Chambers, Covent Garden, London WC2E 8HA)
Launched in 1969 as result of widespread public concern about the gap between rich and poor nations. Its aim is 'political' rather than to give aid, seeking—by contact with politicians and the press, public meetings and publications—to change practices in international trade and government policies, so as to reduce world poverty.

● **Catholic Fund for Overseas Development** (CAFOD, The Garden Close, Stockwell Road, London SW9 9TY)
Welfare bodies of Roman Catholic Church linked together by an organization in Rome called Caritas International. CAFOD is the UK wing

and uses money collected for refugee relief, health education, support for the poor suffering oppression by a wealthy and powerful minority.

● **Tear Fund** (100 Church Road, Teddington, Middlesex TW11 8QE)
Set up in 1967 by Evangelical Alliance an interdenominational Christian organization. Money received is used for both emergency relief and long-term development. Also funds Christian volunteers, who work on medical, agricultural, educational and community development projects. Has child, student and meals sponsorship schemes.

● **World Vision** (Dychurch House, 8 Abington Street, Northampton NN1 2HA)
Interdenominational Christian relief and development agency set up in 1950 as result of work amongst orphans in Korea. Involved in emergency relief after disasters, evangelism, leadership training, child sponsorship and projects to develop self-reliance.

● **Centre for World Development Education** (Regent's College, Inner Circle, Regent's Park, London NW1 4MS)
Educational organization aiming to teach people in UK about development issues and about Britain's links with the Third World. Receives grants from government although is independent of it. Has links with UN organizations.

● **Overseas Development Administration** (Eland House, Stag Place, London SW1E 5DH)
Government department which administers overseas aid programme. Grants, technical aid and loans go to poor Commonwealth countries; aid is also directed through UN organizations and the World Bank.
If you contact any of the above organizations for further information, remember that all except CWDE and ODA are charities and would therefore appreciate a donation towards the cost of sending material, or at the very least a large, stamped, addressed envelope.

WHAT THE BIBLE SAYS ABOUT HELPING THE POOR

God's concern for the victims of poverty, oppression and injustice is evident throughout the Bible, particularly in the laws given to the Israelites in the Old Testament. God's people are clearly told that they must look after the poor.

' "If . . . there is a fellow-Israelite in need . . . do not be selfish and refuse to help him . . . be generous and lend him as much as he needs . . . Give to him freely and unselfishly . . . There will always be some Israelites who are poor and in need, and so I command you to be generous to them." '
(Deuteronomy 15:7–8, 10–11)
God commanded that those in need should be helped and provided for.

★ ★ ★

' "When you gather your crops and fail to bring in some of the corn that you have cut, do not go back for it . . . When you have picked your olives once, do not go back and get those that are left . . . When you have gathered your grapes once, do not go back over the vines a second time . . . they are for the foreigners, orphans, and widows." ' (Deuteronomy 24:19–21)
Farmers were to leave a certain

amount of their crops for the poor to collect, not to grab every last bit of produce for themselves.

★ ★ ★

' "Every third year give the tithe—a tenth of your crops—to the Levites [priests], the foreigners, the orphans, and the widows, so that in every community they will have all they need to eat." ' (Deuteronomy 26:12)
An additional 'tithe' (proportion of income/produce) had to be set aside every third year for the poor.

★ ★ ★

'The Lord says, "The people of Israel have sinned again and again, and for this I will certainly punish them. They sell into slavery honest men who cannot pay their debts, poor men who cannot repay even the price of a pair of sandals. They trample down the weak and helpless and push the poor out of the way . . ." . . . You have oppressed the poor and robbed them of their grain . . . You persecute good men, take bribes, and prevent the poor from getting justice in the courts.' (Amos 2:6–7; 5:11–12)
The prophets announced to the people God's anger when they ignored his laws for caring for the poor.

★ ★ ★

' "Whoever has two shirts must give one to the man who has none, and whoever has food must share it." '
(Luke 3:11)
John the Baptist's teaching included this command for the 'haves' to share with the 'have nots'.

★ ★ ★

'. . . Agabus . . . predicted that a severe famine was about to come over all the earth . . . The disciples decided that each of them would send as much as he could to help their fellow-believers who lived in Judaea.' (Acts 11:28–29)
The early Christians took up special collections when there were special needs.

★ ★ ★

'If a rich person sees his brother in need, yet closes his heart against his brother, how can he claim that he loves God? . . . our love should not be just words and talk; it must be true love, which shows itself in action.'
(1 John 3:17–18)
Helping the poor is a clear obligation for Christians—it is a practical way of showing God's love and concern for people in everyday life.

Bob Geldof has done more than anyone to awaken the conscience and open the wallets of the Western world to the starving in Africa. Through Band Aid's single, 'Do They Know It's Christmas?', followed by Live Aid and Sport Aid events, he has helped raise £70 million for Africa. In 1986 he received a knighthood in recognition for his humanitarian work.

world, and there is sufficient wealth to buy grain, people in the poorer countries face starvation.

The poor world also needs *gifts* of money to break the cycles of deprivation, and not *loans* which have to be repaid to the rich countries with interest. This need not be impossible: one-half of 1 per cent of one year's world military expenditure would pay for all the farm equipment needed to increase food production and approach self-sufficiency in food-deficit, low-income countries by 1990.

Attitudes in world faiths

The Jews look to the Old Testament Law and Prophets as their authority, and so they are concerned for the poor. Every Jewish community has an organized system of poor relief, and members are taxed to provide this. A Jew is supposed to give up to the point where he would need charity himself if he gave any more! The tax amounted to about one-fifth of his capital and one-fifth of his profits each year. The needs of the poor were to be met, and a person had to start by providing for the needy in his own family. Moses Maimonides, the leading medieval Jewish philosopher, said that there were eight degrees of charity: the lowest was when a man lends to the poor with a glum face; the highest was when a loan or job is given to the poor so that he can support himself.

Zakat (charity) is the third obligation of **Islam**. Two and a half per cent of savings and 10 per cent of the value of jewellery is given annually to charity. In Muslim countries, this 'poor due' is collected by the government, but in other countries it is generally informally given to those in need. It is to be given to a deserving fellow human being, a new convert to Islam, a traveller or a person with debts. The percentages quoted are the minimum. Allah himself will reward those who give more.

The idea behind *zakat* is that it fosters a spirit of sacrifice and rids people of selfishness. This prepares them for greater sacrifices which may be demanded, and it redistributes the wealth of society in such a way that society can function properly. Muhammad himself was an orphan and knew how important charity could be.

Basing their beliefs on the teaching in the Bible, **Christians** would summarize their reasons for giving to the poor as follows:
- Giving to the poor is **love in action**. It is not enough to feel sympathy for someone in need. The poor need food, clothing, shelter, medicine, hope for the future . . .
- Giving to the poor is **to meet with Jesus again**. Jesus said that when we give to people in need, it is the same as giving to him.
- Giving to the poor is **fighting against evil**. Poverty is often caused by injustice and corruption, and Christians are encouraged to fight against such evils wherever they find them.

Discussion topics

1 'Charity begins at home.' Do you agree? Do you think the UK has enough problems of its own without having to help struggling countries overseas?

2 One in three Americans and one in five Britons suffer from obesity (being grossly overweight) while close on 500 million people in the world are severely undernourished. Is the world food problem one of a shortage of resources or selfish distribution?

3 Do you agree that 'poverty is powerlessness'?

UNIT 20

HEALTH

In the West we are so used to a normally healthy and energetic life-style that we often forget what conditions were like some 200 years ago. Progress in raising health standards in Europe and North America since 1800 has been staggering.

World health

Despite the improvements in the West, much of the world—mainly the poor developing nations—still have to live in what we might call 'pre-1800 conditions'. Health is no longer a local or national concern only—it needs tackling on a worldwide scale, for four major reasons:

● **Mobility** The world has effectively become much 'smaller' since air travel made it possible to cross the globe in a few hours. Someone from a place where a certain disease still exists can therefore travel and carry it to an area where it has been eradicated. The infection can then spread very rapidly in the new area because no natural resistance exists any longer and no precautions have been taken against the disease. This can also happen by visitors from the Western world introducing a disease such as measles—simply an inconvenience in their own country—to another part of the world (for example, South America) where it is fatal to hundreds of people.

● **Co-operation** Diseases such as malaria, which is carried by the mosquito, can be controlled only 'at source' by aerial spraying. This has to be done across national boundaries —the insects do not recognize a frontier! Only where there is international agreement is such a programme possible. Other diseases —such as those caused by diet deficiency—are so great a problem that they can be dealt with only if

the wealthier nations pool their resources. One positive example of recent international co-operation (achieved by the World Health Organization and collaborating countries) has been the successful eradication of smallpox. The amount of money needed each year to deal with world health problems has been calculated at £7,000 million. This seems an impossibly large sum—until one realizes that for the price of one jet fighter (£13 million), about 40,000 village pharmacies could be set up. Less than half a day's worldwide military expenditure would be needed to conquer river-blindness, a disease which blights the lives of millions in the Third World.

● **Injustice** Why should the

Western world have such high standards of health while people in Third World countries suffer diseases due to malnutrition, poor sanitation and water supplies, and inadequate medical services? Many people feel that it is unjust that someone's life should be crippled or ended early simply because they were born in the 'wrong' place. In the UK in 1980, for example, there was one doctor to every 650 persons and one nurse to every 140, while in Ethiopia there is one doctor to every 69,390 persons, and one nurse to every 5,910. The sense of injustice is heightened when it seems that the wealthy nations of the world will not give the poorer nations the chance to help themselves (see Unit 19, Poverty).

● **The Brandt Report, 1980**
'Most people in the Third World are living much longer today than they were only two decades ago. In sub-Saharan Africa . . . life expectancy is still very low: the average is only about 45 years. But in large parts of South and East Asia, in North Africa and the Middle East, people can expect to live 10 to 15 years longer. Much of this has been achieved by controlling communicable diseases, including cholera and malaria . . .

'But poor health is still the likely fate of much of the Third World. The population censuses of 1970–71 showed that death rates were not declining as fast as expected . . . There are still countries in Africa where one child in four does not survive until its first birthday.

Health hazards in the Third World

❛ "Once you are in Kirillapone shanty you never get out", is an accepted saying among the 2,000 people living in Sri Lanka's biggest shanty. It lies on the outskirts of Colombo on a congested 2-hectare site where the physical problems are typical of many third world communities —flimsy housing, inadequate water supply and virtually non-existent sanitation. Over 450 families are crowded into the area

which is bordered on two sides by a polluted storm water channel and on the other by a disease-ridden canal. One of the biggest health risks is a set of latrines standing in one corner of the site, virtually unused because of years of poor maintenance. On the perimeter there are four stand pipes serving the needs of the entire population. And the shanty homes are separated by a maze of narrow pathways which become a quagmire during the monsoon rains . . . ❜
New Civil Engineer

Blindness affects 30 to 40 million people in the Third World and threatens many tens of millions more . . . No one knows how many people are undernourished and hungry, but . . . the number could be more than one-fifth of the whole Third World, or 500–600 million people . . .

'In virtually half the world water supplies are uncertain. Four out of five people living in the rural areas of developing countries do not have reasonable access to even relatively unpolluted water . . . Between 20 and 25 million children below the age of five die every year in developing countries, and a third of these deaths are from diarrhoea caught from polluted water . . .

'Improving health requires efforts far beyond medical care; it is closely linked with food and nutrition, with employment and income distribution and with the international economy.'

● **Language** If you have been abroad on holiday, you will be aware of the communication problems that can arise just in everyday life. In the field of medicine, it is vitally important to standardize language so that co-operation is possible: common names and common constituents for drugs need to be agreed so that they can be used safely internationally: common terms are needed for injuries, diseases and causes of death, so that meaningful statistics of trends can be kept and compared for different parts of the world.

Why is it that the Western world has seen such a great improvement in health standards since 1800? If we look simply at the development of medicine, health education, the improvement of food supplies and living conditions, we miss the point. All these were made possible only *because the West became wealthy* through industrialization and could afford to use its wealth to raise living standards by these means.

Health is much more than the use of drugs and medicine to cure disease. Health is prevention of disease, too—it is knowing how to live so that disease does not start. It also involves:
● a person's relationships with his surroundings—a healthy environment is likely to lead to good health;

● a person's relationships with others—if he feels lonely or rejected by his community, or if he is bitter and resentful, he may become ill;
● a person's relationship with himself—there is more to health than a healthy body: happiness and peace of mind are fundamental, too, and they cannot be bought.

Social and environmental factors

Christian doctors working at Vellore Medical College in India found that 70 per cent of the diseases they treated could have been prevented—that is, by changing the conditions in which their patients lived. If standards of health are to be raised in poor countries, there is a need to improve a whole range of social and environmental conditions:

● **Diet** Disease frequently results from lack of food (in general) or lack of specific kinds of food. People who are weakened through an inadequate diet find it very difficult to resist infection. Provision of food depends on either having land to grow it on or having money to buy it—many people in the Third World have neither. A high birth rate and large families mean more mouths to feed.

● **Water supply** Many diseases of the Third World are caused by the lack of a safe, reliable, piped water supply. High standards of hygiene are almost impossible to maintain, and water-borne diseases are spread by the widespread use of infected pools, streams and rivers for drinking and washing.

● **Housing and sanitation** Standards of housing in developing countries are generally poor, with none of the 'mod cons' the West takes for granted. Migration from rural areas to shanty towns on the outskirts of big cities is an enormous problem—conditions in these are overcrowded, squalid and extremely unhealthy. Drainage, sanitation and the removal of refuse are normally quite inadequate, leading to widespread disease.

● **Education** Increasing standards of literacy is vital in improving world health. Dosage instructions on a batch of tablets or descriptions of how to sterilize a baby's bottle mean nothing if you cannot read. Even the success of family planning methods depends on people being taught why and how to use them on a regular basis. Matters of health and hygiene are matters of education.

The professional factor

If you become ill in a developing country, it can be very difficult to obtain the help of a professional doctor. Due to the lack of resources and facilities, few people can train to be doctors in poor countries. Often those who *are* able to train do so overseas, and it is then a temptation for them to seek a practice in a wealthy country rather than face the

Only if a baby's weight increases regularly will he or she grow up healthily. This is a chart of an African baby. Keep one of a baby you know and compare.

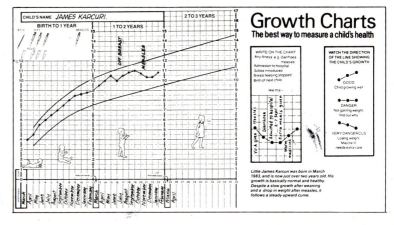

Growth Charts
The best way to measure a child's health

Little James Karcuri was born in March 1983, and is now just over two years old. His growth is basically normal and healthy. Despite a slow growth after weaning and a drop in weight after measles, it follows a steady upward curve.

problems and poverty of home. Thirty-five per cent of the doctors in British hospitals have come from other countries; 50 per cent of the medical graduates in Pakistan and Sri Lanka leave every year for other countries. The poorest countries therefore find it very difficult to provide medical services, despite their desperate need for professional help.

Faced with this problem, some of the poorer countries have adopted an alternative approach. 'Lower-level' medical care is placed in the hands of less highly-qualified people. In Malawi and Tanzania, medical assistants (not as highly trained as doctors) are put in charge of health centres in rural districts. In China, keen peasants are trained as health workers when agricultural work is slack: they learn the importance of clean water and sanitation, how to undertake an immunization

In England and Wales, there is one doctor for approximately 600 people; in Haiti, there is one doctor for every 11,000 people, and in Rwanda, the figure is one to 39,000. In many Third World countries, a doctor may visit an outlying clinic once a week or once a month, and specialist help for any serious complaint may be several hundred miles away.

ORGANIZING FOR HEALTH

The problem of world health has so concerned members of the United Nations Organization that they have set up specific bodies to try to help. The major ones are the World Health Organization (WHO), based in Geneva, and the Food and Agriculture Organization (FAO), based in Rome.

The World Health Organization was set up in 1948 to protect and promote world health. It accepted an understanding of health as the state of complete physical, mental and social well-being, and not merely the absence of disease. It believed that the enjoyment of the highest available standard of health is one of the fundamental rights of every human being, and that the health of all peoples underlies the attainment of peace and security.

The work of the WHO can be summarized as follows:
● to give help to countries requesting it in setting up health programmes (training nurses, nutrition, family planning, water supply, sanitation), training health workers, and medical research;
● to monitor contagious disease—telex messages are sent to all countries if there is the threat of an epidemic;
● to spread information about health;

● to supervise the production of drugs and ensure that they reach a satisfactory standard;
● to supervise and amend international health regulations so as to stop the spread of disease (for example, demanding vaccination certificates from travellers if there is an outbreak of some disease);
● to inform all countries about unsafe drugs;
● to collect and share information about research into such areas as pollution and health, cancer, heart disease and mental illness;
● to collect and share statistics and information about infant mortality, birth and death rates in different countries;
● to give financial and manpower resources to projects trying to eradicate diseases such as malaria, tuberculosis, leprosy, yellow fever and cholera.

The Food and Agriculture Organization was set up in 1945. All 144 member nations pay shares into the organization in proportion to their national prosperity. The annual budget runs at about £100 million.

The organization has several aims: to raise the level of nutrition and standards of living, to improve production and distribution of food and to better the conditions of rural

populations to allow the world economy to expand and to bring about freedom from hunger. In order to fulfil its aims, the FAO seeks to do the following:
● to increase food production from rivers, seas and land by projects such as land and water development, immunization of cattle, eradication of pests and development of industries such as forestry;
● to help countries to finance new agricultural development by working with the World Bank and other financiers;
● to collect information about food and agriculture from all over the world to assist future planning;
● to provide an 'early warning system' to areas likely to suffer famine, and to plan for a renewal of agriculture;
● to provide a forum for discussing agricultural problems;
● to sponsor the World Food Programme—this commenced work in 1963 to shift food surpluses to areas of need. It also feeds people working on rural development projects, feeds school-children, encourages land settlement by giving help until a farmer can become self-supporting and feeds volunteers establishing social services.

programme and how to give simple medicines. The Chinese have also accepted the saying of the late Chairman Mao: 'Involve everyone in caring for his own health and for his neighbour's.' In applying this principle, whole communities have worked together—for example, to eradicate pests which have caused disease.

Christian medical missions

In many developing countries, the first medical help was provided by Christian mission hospitals and clinics. Christians believe that, just as Jesus was concerned for the *whole* person (body, mind and spirit), so they should be involved in helping to bring about physical, mental and spiritual health.

As Christian preachers entered the countries we now call the Third World, they found that many people were suffering from disease, malnutrition, blindness, illiteracy and poverty. They responded by showing practical, loving help. Medical, educational, technical, literacy and agricultural works were established to go alongside their work of preaching about Jesus. This is still an important feature of Christian missions today.

The Christian approach to health and healing is based upon three principles drawn from the Bible's teaching (see also Unit 14, Medicine):

● **Preventative medicine** Many diseases are caused through excess and can be prevented if people moderate their behaviour. The New Testament encourages Christians to avoid excesses which lead to ill-health. The Jewish laws in the Old Testament also made Christians aware of many health regulations (about food, water, sewage disposal and quarantine) which, if followed, led to freedom from disease. A Christian regards his life as belonging to God and wants to keep it (as far as possible) fit and healthy; he believes that others should have the chance to learn the principles of healthy living too.

● **Curative medicine** Most Christians recognize both medical and non-medical healing as ways that God can use to cure people of illness. Medical healing is based on a knowledge of how natural healing takes place and how the body works; non-medical healing takes place when a person is made 'miraculously' well without medical intervention.

Luke, who wrote one of the New Testament Gospels, was a doctor who practised medical healing. The Bible also records many examples of non-medical healing. None of Jesus' twelve disciples had any medical training, but they were sent out to heal. Healing services take place regularly at the present time in some Christian churches.

● **The whole person** Christians believe that Jesus' message is relevant to a person's material *and* spiritual well-being. Jesus said that he came to heal, but also to forgive sins, and to help the poor and free the oppressed. Throughout his life he taught that a new relationship with God would make people *spiritually* healthy—he freed people from the 'disease' of sin, at the same time as healing their bodies of sickness. His followers were to 'heal the sick', as a 'sign' while preaching 'the good news of the kingdom'.

UNIT 21

POPULATION

It is not easy for us to imagine the primitive life-style of 10,000 years ago. People lived in caves, several families together (see also Unit 3, The Family). The men went off to hunt; when the hunt was successful, the animal carcass was brought back to the cave for the women to cook, and for the skin to be used for clothing. The women not only looked after their families' needs, but they went 'hunting' too—for seeds which could be crushed and turned into crude 'flour' for their primitive cooking.

The population was small (estimates put the total world population at this time at about 5 million). Two square miles of countryside were needed to support one person, but even so, hunting was not always successful. The food supply was unreliable and the caves unhealthy. Life was brief. There seems to have been a natural means of birth control: only the small families survived, because large families quickly suffered starvation.

Then, some 9,000 years ago, there was a 'revolution' which led to a large increase in population. It was the Neolithic revolution—the discovery of farming.

The idea dawned on the womenfolk that, if they dug up the plants which gave them seeds and planted them in one place, they would not have to travel so far or search for the seeds. They may also have discovered by accident that, if some of the seeds fell into the ground, they developed new plants in the succeeding year. However it came about, the idea of plots of ground for the sowing of seed was born. This development meant that it was necessary to move out of the caves into primitive huts by the fields, so that wild animals could be driven away from the crops, and weeding out of unwanted plants could be done. The huts were crude, but they were healthier than the caves.

The cultivation of grain was followed by the domestication of animals: first, the goat was tamed, then the sheep, pig and cow. The result of this change was an increase in the food supply and an improvement in health. Families were able to produce more food than they themselves needed. A food surplus made it possible for some people in a community to specialize in activities unconnected with farming, such as pottery, carpentry and metalwork. More substantial dwellings were built. All this contributed to a higher standard of living. The result of all these developments was an increase in population.

Round two

This general pattern of life did not change for thousands of years. There were overall improvements in living standards; from time to time an outbreak of plague would decimate the population. But all the power which was used was 'muscle' power —by man or animal. This was all changed by another better-known revolution, which began in Britain around 1750—the Industrial Revolution.

The Industrial Revolution was based on steam power. Britain gradually changed from being a farming-based society to a manufacturing society. Because it was now possible to produce the same goods as had been made previously much more cheaply, there was a rapid increase in wealth. The wealth was used for new machinery, to build roads and railways, to import food from other countries, to improve sanitation and water supplies, and to sponsor medical research so that disease could be brought under control. For the first time, it was possible for people to avoid starvation because food could be purchased and distributed.

As health improved with the rising standard of living, fewer children died in infancy and life expectancy increased. People were encouraged by the fact that a large family no longer involved the threat of starvation, but rather that larger families meant more potential workers and more money. Soon the birth rate overtook the death rate and the population increased dramatically.

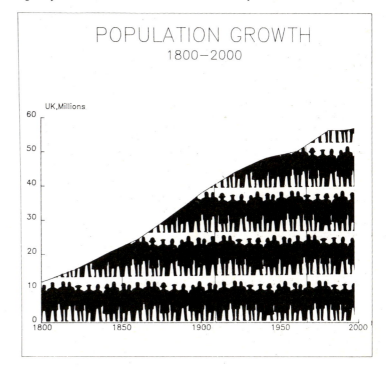

POPULATION GROWTH
1800–2000

UK, Millions

After a time, the birth rate in an industrial society begins to slow down:

- Large families are no longer needed to increase wealth.
- Material things which national wealth brings are not available if there are too many children to be looked after.
- Machines replace people at various jobs, so that too many children may worsen the unemployment problem.
- Effective methods of birth control have been developed and are widely used.

'Late developers'

The Industrial Revolution spread to other parts of the world from its base in north-west Europe. Industrialized countries have now reached the stage where the increase in the birth rate is slowing down. In fact, some are worried that they now have negative population growth and a declining population.

However, there is a great problem in other parts of the world to which industrialization has spread more recently. Population is now increasing very rapidly in Third World countries, and in some the birth rate shows no signs of slowing down as it has done in Western, industrial nations.

This is because the Third World countries where the dramatic increase is taking place already had a large population when industrialization started. At the beginning of the Industrial Revolution in Britain, the population was 9 million. When India began to industrialize after gaining independence in 1948, the population was 600 million. All the wealth obtained through industrialization is needed simply to provide the population with basic necessities, to try to alleviate the worse effects of absolute poverty and to meet the huge costs of rapid urbanization.

The results

Thomas Malthus (1766–1834) was brought up in England in a wealthy landowner's family. His father believed that a perfect society could be brought about in which everyone would be happy; Thomas believed

Hong Kong is the world's most densely populated country. Ninety per cent of its 4.2 million population live on the 14 per cent of its land area which is urbanized. The price of land necessitates high-rise building.

that disaster, not happiness, awaited mankind. The reason for this, as he saw it, was that the world's food supply would not be adequate for the growing population.

Malthus worked out that the world's food supply could only be increased *by the same amount* every few years, but that the world's population would increase *by the same proportion* every few years. The population would therefore outstrip the food supply and the human race would face death through starvation, disease and war. He explained his ideas in a book called *An Essay on the Principles of Population*, published in 1798.

For a long time it seemed that Malthus was wrong. Developments

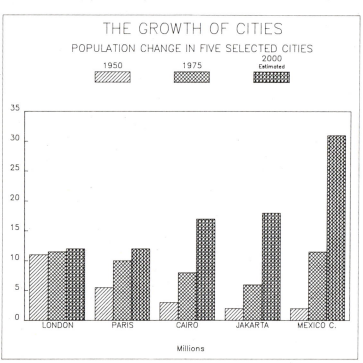

THE GROWTH OF CITIES
POPULATION CHANGE IN FIVE SELECTED CITIES

1950	1975	2000 Estimated

Millions

in agricultural techniques have led to vastly increased crop production. Migration from the older, industrialized countries to other parts of the world—such as Canada, Australia and South Africa—resulted in an increase in cultivated land. The growth in population worldwide then became so great that many people began to believe that Malthus's predictions would soon come true. But of course now the reaction has set in. Governments have introduced massive birth control programmes in countries such as China and India. The predictions of high population increases have frightened people into organizing such campaigns.

The immediate observable effects of rapid population growth are:

● **Overcrowding** In the UK there are 230 people to every square kilometre of land, and people talk about it being difficult to 'get away from it all'. In poorer countries where there is urban overcrowding, it is impossible for everyone to be adequately housed. Shanty towns mushroom on the outskirts of large cities. Overcrowding has undesirable side-effects such as crime and violence. In a rural area, the farms become too small to support a family adequately.

● **Food shortage** The population of Third World countries is growing so rapidly that their food production needed to be increased by 75 per cent between 1965 and 1980, and by 225 per cent between 1965 and 2000. Crop failures, droughts and floods continue to affect food supplies in developing countries, and hundreds of thousands live daily with the threat of starvation. The problem of fair distribution also influences food shortages (see Unit 19, Poverty).

● **Use of resources** An increasing population makes increasing demands on all kinds of resources, such as water, fuel and minerals.

● **Social deprivation** As population increases, it is very difficult for the government of a country to keep pace with the provision of social services. Education, health and welfare services are costly, and many Third World governments cannot afford to provide them adequately.

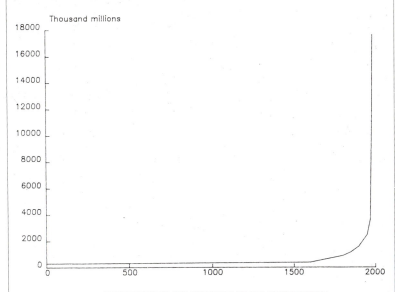

WORLD POPULATION

INCREASE SINCE THE BEGINNING OF THE FIRST CENTURY

● **Simple facts**
There are 3 births every 2 seconds, 90 births each minute, 200,000 births each day.
World population doubles every 35 years.

● **'Million' cities**
In 1935, there were 56 cities with more than a million inhabitants;
in 1960, there were 100.
In 2000, there will probably be about 500.

DIFFERENTIAL GROWTH RATES
(based on 1983 figures)

Area	Existing population (in millions)	Growth rate (% per year)
UK	56	N/A
USA	234	0.7
USSR	273	0.7
Australia	15	1.0
Ethiopia	41	2.6
Uganda	14	3.3
Mexico	75	2.3
Libya	3	4.1

? What general trends are shown?
? What problems may arise from the imbalance between population growth rates?

'The growth of population at rates between 2 and 3 per cent per annum will produce a doubling of population in 25 to 35 years . . . The decline in fertility during the 1980s and 1990s is not likely to make a great difference to the total numbers in the year 2000 but it is decisive to what happens after that . . . World population could stabilize at levels anywhere between 8 and 15 billion in the course of the next century . . . The populations of most countries in the developing world are likely to reach at least twice their present size . . . India will have at least 1.2 billion inhabitants.'
The Brandt Report, 1980

● **Imbalance** The wealthier, industrialized countries can generate money needed for social services. This widens the gap between rich and poor, as Third World countries cannot afford to provide for their people in this way.

Solutions?

Short-term solutions to the world population problem aim at alleviation, and put a priority on improving food production. Agricultural scientists produced high-yielding strains of wheat and rice in what has been called the 'Green Revolution' of the mid-60s to the mid-70s.

The introduction and use of machinery and modern farming methods have not been without their problems however. They have contributed to unemployment in the

---

6 Conservation of wild life so necessary to human well-being is pointless unless man succeeds in conserving himself. For this he must enter into absolute control of his birth rate. Without this he will lose his birthright. 9

Church of England Report: Man in his Living Environment

Third World by replacing people on the land by machines. Spare parts and servicing of machines may not be easy to provide locally either. Poorer nations find it difficult to afford fertilizers, for example, or to finance vast irrigation schemes to ensure a reliable water supply for their crops. It is important that technology introduced should be 'appropriate' to the area concerned.

Another solution which has been suggested is the long-term one of educating people in family planning techniques so that the population does not increase at so great a rate.

A Christian perspective

There is no direct guidance in the Bible about population control on an overcrowded planet. It was written at a time when the total world population was only 200–300 million and present-day problems were

unknown. In a predominantly agricultural society, large families were seen as a blessing from God, because there were many pairs of hands to cope with the work.

Christians place great emphasis on family and community life because of its obvious importance throughout the Bible. The importance of helping others in need is also clearly taught. Not only is love for one's neighbour part of both Old and New Testament law, but failure to help those in need is a reason for experiencing God's judgement.

The two principles of family life and care for others have led Roman Catholics to make a strong response to the population crisis. They teach that artificial methods of birth control are morally wrong, because they are unnatural ways of frustrating God's purpose for sexual intercourse. The Catholic Church believes that the problem of overpopulation is therefore not to be solved through birth control, but through self control, the equitable sharing of resources and efforts to increase food production.

Other Christians express their beliefs about birth control in terms of some or all of the following points:
● Sexual intercourse is to deepen a married couple's relationship, not solely for the procreation of children.
● It is irresponsible to bring unwanted children into an already overpopulated world.
● Contraception is a tool to help us manage the world's resources.
● A couple should be open to the possibility of having children (unless there is some very good reason for not doing so) but should be free to use artificial contraceptive aids on particular occasions.
● Abortion (except in very rare cases) is an unacceptable form of birth control.

Discussion topics

1 Other methods (besides voluntary limitation by birth control and social pressure) of controlling world population have been suggested:
● sterilization (with financial incentives);
● abortion of unwanted children;
● removal of child allowances;
● financial rewards for couples with

late, few or no children;
● encouraging women to pursue interesting careers and not have families;
● increasing pensions so that old people will not have to rely on the support of their children.
What do you think about each of these?

2 How would you feel if legislation were introduced limiting the size of families or compelling you to lower your standard of living in the interests of the Third World?

3 Some developing countries are actively encouraging population increase; others see birth control as 'the white man's trick'. Why do you think these attitudes have developed? Can anything be done about them?

4 Does the threat of an overpopulated planet running out of resources worry you? What do you intend to do about it?

UNIT 22

LITERACY

Imagine you are on a touring holiday abroad and you arrive in a busy city. You cannot understand what people are saying, and the writing on the street signs is unlike anything you have ever seen before. You don't know where to park because you've no idea which sign means 'Parking'. Nobody can understand you when you ask for directions to the city centre. You hope that the city uses the familiar male and female figures rather than words on toilet doors.

Getting something to eat is not so difficult because even though you cannot read words or work out prices in the shops, you can point to what you want and trust that the assistant gives you the right change. You return to your parked car and find an official form tucked under the windscreen wiper. It looks like a parking ticket, but you can't read what it says, and nobody round about can explain to you what to do.

It probably would not take you long to become extremely worried, upset and frustrated in this situation. You may decide that it is best to get away from the place as quickly and quietly as possible and find somewhere where there are fewer worries. You may even become so frustrated that you take it out on a passer-by who cannot talk to you.

What has just been described is the problem of illiteracy—the results of being unable to read the written word or to communicate through writing.

What does it mean?

How poor does a person have to be at reading and writing to be called 'illiterate'? In the UK, it means that a person can read no better than an average child aged between seven and nine years old. A person who can read as well as the average seven year old is said to have a 'reading

age' of seven; a book or magazine which can be read by an average nine year old—but not a younger child—is said to have a 'reading age' of nine.

The reading age of a book or magazine depends on the length of the sentences and the length of the words. People with reading difficulties cannot understand long sentences, and have trouble trying to read long, unusual words. Books with a 'low' reading age, therefore, have short sentences and short words, and books with a 'high' reading age have longer sentences and a higher percentage of long

words.

You can use the length of sentences and words to find out the reading age of a book, magazine, instructions (e.g. on a food packet) or official form:
● Choose styles of writing as varied as possible.
● Select three 100-word passages from each piece of writing.
● Count up the number of *syllables* in each passage and find the average (giving an indication of the length of words).
● Count the number of *sentences* in each passage, making an estimate of

Chart for calculating reading age

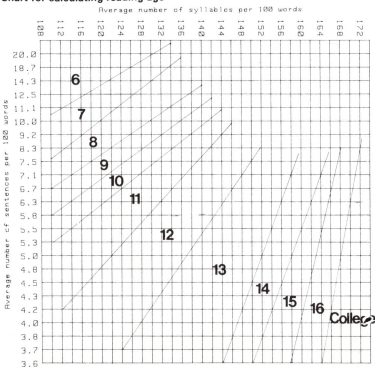

Here are some results found by other people:

	Reading age
Articles in *Daily Mirror* and *The Sun* newspapers	9–16
Instructions on soup packets	10–17
National Insurance Guide for women	10–17
Claims for industrial injury	10–18
Family allowance for immigrants (in English)	13–18
Highway Code	13+
Income tax form	15–18
Family Income Supplement form	16+
Average trades union form	17

? What problems might people with reading difficulties have with some of the above?

the fraction left over, and again find the average (showing how long the sentences are).

● Find out where the two figures (for each passage) intersect on the chart. The reading age of the piece of writing can then be read off between six and sixteen years old or college standard.

The extent of illiteracy

Is a reading age of seven to nine years old a realistic figure for literacy? People with a reading age of ten would have difficulty with many of the important documents listed in the last section. In this respect, the UK differs from the standards adopted by other nations.

The United Nations Educational, Scientific and Cultural Organization (UNESCO) believes that the reading age for literacy should be thirteen years. In a statement made in 1962 (was it designed to test understanding?), the Director-General said, 'A person is literate

---

❛ It is a scandal that so many men and women should still be illiterate in the present age, and it is a dangerous contradiction that we find a human society so organized (or rather, disorganized) that some nations are able to boast that 30% of their young people are receiving higher education while in others only 3% of the actual population can read or write.**❜**
Director-General, UNESCO

Warning signs may be conveying important messages but they are worthless to the person who cannot read.

when he has acquired the essential knowledge and skills which enable him to engage in all those activities in which literacy is required for the effective functioning in his group and community, and whose attainments in reading, writing and arithmetic make it possible for him to continue to use those skills towards his own and towards his community's development.'

Using that kind of definition, we soon discover that illiteracy is a huge world problem. It is also a growing problem: with the world's increasing population, the number of illiterates has been rising steadily. There are now 150 million more illiterate people in the world than there were in 1950.

Various projects to help the

THE STORY OF WRITING

Written communication was first attempted through simple pictures between 4,000 and 5,000 years ago in ancient Sumeria and Egypt. Below are examples of how letters are thought to have developed from pictures or symbols:

● An ox, or *Aleph*, was drawn, representing an *object*
The symbol was gradually simplified
Its final form was a letter of the alphabet, representing a *sound* (the first sound in the word 'Aleph')   A

● A snake, or *Nahas*, was drawn
It was simplified to a symbol
Eventually the letter representing its first sound was drawn   N

● A man's head was called 'Resh' and was drawn
Its symbol became
The letter which came to represent its first sound was   R

Aleph, *nahas* and *resh* are words from biblical Hebrew; the script used in the symbols is much older than Hebrew, and underlies this particular group of languages.

In some languages, the picture came to stand for a syllable and not a sound. This happened in Chinese and Japanese—in these languages, there are many more syllables than sounds, so there are many more symbols in their writing.

Writing was a very important development in the ancient world, because it enabled kings to keep records, and priests to put laws into written form that would not change. Members of the community who could write became very powerful.

UNESCO

UNESCO is the United Nations agency which tackles problems in education, science and culture, in the belief that such work will lead to lasting peace. Twenty states formed UNESCO in 1946, stating that 'since wars begin in the minds of men, it is in the minds of men that the defences of peace must be constructed'.

The agency started life by collecting and sending books to re-equip bombed libraries, sorting out and distributing educational equipment for teaching purposes, and by linking together schools in different countries. There are now 142 member states, each of whom contributes to a central fund. They decide together how the money is to be spent, and the Paris headquarters puts their wishes into effect.

UNESCO has wide cultural interests, and was well known for its work in helping to save the ancient Egyptian temples from being submerged by the waters of the Nile behind the new Aswan Dam. Its scientific interests include the sponsorship of a European centre for nuclear research.

Within the educational programme are many schemes for improving the level of literacy, by allocating funds for literacy projects and by making the needs widely known, to raise support and finance. The secretariat of UNESCO keeps statistics of literacy and publications worldwide. These show, for example, that in 1979 the Bible was the most translated work, with thirty new translations made in that year; the works of Shakespeare came a close second (twenty-nine) followed by the works of Karl Marx and Dostoyevsky (twenty-six).

The UK left UNESCO in 1985 because the Government believed that the organization was being controlled by countries which did not contribute much finance to it. Most were poor nations of the Third World which needed the help of the organization. Do you think the UK should have left?

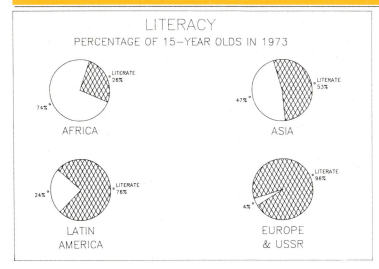

LITERACY
PERCENTAGE OF 15—YEAR OLDS IN 1973

AFRICA — LITERATE 26%, 74°

ASIA — LITERATE 53%, 47°

LATIN AMERICA — LITERATE 76%, 24°

EUROPE & USSR — LITERATE 96%, 4°

LITERACY IS RELATED TO NUMBERS OF PEOPLE IN EDUCATION:
Compare these 1982 figures which show % of age group in education

	Primary Ed		Secondary Ed	Higher Ed
	Boys	Girls		
UK	*102	103	83	19
THAILAND	98	94	29	22
MOROCCO	98	62	28	6
PAKISTAN	57	31	14	2
UGANDA	69	51	8	1
SUDAN	61	43	18	2

*The numbers in school sometimes exceed the birthrate for a given age group because of such factors as immigration, failure to record birth.

illiterate have been established. Those who get involved do so from a variety of motives. They may believe that illiteracy is:

● **a moral issue**—it is wrong that people should be mentally stunted because they cannot read;

● **a political issue**—it is socially unjust that some people should be able to read while others cannot;

● **a development issue**—a high percentage of illiterate people in a country hinders its progress and keeps living standards low.

Many charities such as Oxfam, War on Want and Christian Aid use a proportion of the money they receive for literacy work in underdeveloped countries.

Literacy campaigns

We do not know exactly how many adults in the UK are illiterate, because most people who cannot read or write are embarrassed to admit it. When someone comes forward to ask to be taught to read, it is usually because they have seen a programme or advert on television, or because a social worker or sympathetic employer understands their problem and has encouraged them to ask for help.

People who are willing to teach reading are often organized by the

───────────────────

❛ Hunger for education is no less debasing than hunger for food. An illiterate is a person with an undernourished mind. ❜
Pope Paul VI

───────────────────

local education service. They may visit homes to give individual tuition, or set up a local centre where individuals or small groups can come. Some groups exist specifically to help immigrants to learn to read and write English.

However, there are not many books available to teach *adults* to read—large letters, short words and short sentences are features of children's books and adults obviously do not want to learn to read from books designed for children in an infants' school! Volunteers therefore have to write a lot of their own material—for example, about do-it-yourself projects, where to go when help is needed, about local sport and events. With encouragement and patience, most non-readers are able to learn to read so that they can cope in all everyday situations where reading and writing skills will be demanded.

Christians have always been concerned to help people to read, so that they can understand for themselves God's message to mankind as written in the Bible.

In the eighteenth century, Christian businessman Robert Raikes started the first Sunday school in Gloucester to teach poor children to read, so that they could read the Bible. There has always been an educational emphasis in the work of Christian missions, and involvement in translating the Bible into 'the language of the people'.

When people become Christians, it has often given them the motivation they need to want to read, so that they can read the Bible and Christian books. Christianity and literacy have gone together.

Christians have been influenced by other factors too. First, the conviction that it is wrong for people to remain illiterate so that their development as human beings is held back. Second, Christians have felt strongly that there is a need for *good* reading material to be produced. It is not enough to teach people to read; they have to be able to practise and develop their reading skills.

Assignments and discussion topics

1 Devise a simple introduction to life in Britain (short words, short sentences) for an immigrant who had recently learned to read English.
2 'To be able to read and write . . . is to recover confidence in oneself and to discover that one can progress along with others.' Do you agree?
3 'The pen is mightier than the sword.' What do you think this means? Do you agree?

UNIT 23

NATURAL DISASTERS

A severe earthquake in a city is a major disaster. Violent earth movements lasting only a few seconds cause buildings to collapse, rip huge holes in roads and railways and fracture gas and water mains. Inflammable material spills and fires start. Power and communication lines are cut. Dead bodies litter the streets or are buried in the rubble; survivors stagger about in a dazed and shocked condition. In a coastal city, the disaster might not even stop there. A tidal wave, or *tsunami*, could be set off by the upheaval and flood in over the stricken city.

This kind of disaster has happened a number of times. In 1755 in Lisbon, Portugal, 30,000 people died in an earthquake. In 1932, 100,000 people died in an earthquake which struck Tokyo, Japan. The earthquake near Naples in southern Italy in November 1980 left over 10,000 dead, 8,000 injured and 350,000 homeless.

Earthquakes are not the only kind of natural disaster which can destroy a city. The eruption of the volcano Vesuvius wiped out the Roman cities of Pompeii and Herculaneum in AD 79; 26,000 on the West Indian island of Martinique died when Mont Pelée erupted in 1902. Darwin, on Australia's northern coast, was destroyed by a cyclone in 1974 on Christmas Day.

There are other natural disasters which are equally destructive of human life: floods and droughts take longer to have an effect, but they claim just as many lives as do tropical storms, earthquakes or volcanoes.

All such violent natural occurrences are called 'acts of God', because at one time people believed that the gods were directly responsible for such happenings. Even in the twentieth century, they are largely unpredictable and there is little which man can do to protect himself against them, even though we now know more about the causes, such as geological faults in the earth's crust.

Emergency relief

If such a disaster were to take place in a city in the UK, it would not be very long before rescue services arrived to help. The fire brigade, police and ambulance services would be on the scene as soon as they realized what had happened. The trapped and injured would be taken to hospitals outside the affected area, and the main roads cleared as quickly as possible of bodies, cars and débris. Welfare services would move in to provide food for those who remained in the city.

The government would appoint a minister to co-ordinate all the rescue services and to bring in the armed forces if necessary. With their help, emergency water and telephone services would be set up, guards would be put on commercial premises where security was important, sewage disposal would be arranged, emergency lighting supplied and heavy equipment would move in to shift fallen masonry. Other emergency organizations, such as the Red Cross, would supply tents and blankets for both the homeless and the rescue workers.

Disaster it may be, but the national emergency services would be able to cope with it. When it was over, government grants, national appeals and insurance money where it is payable (not all policies cover 'acts of God', as they still call them in the insurance world) would make funds available for reconstruction.

By contrast, most Third World countries are subject to large-scale natural disasters, but few have the wealth to provide emergency services to cope with the situation. Imagine an earthquake taking place in a Third World city, surrounded by the normal shanty town. There would be an appalling death toll because of the overcrowding typical of such a city. The poverty of the country would make a co-ordinated rescue operation impossible. It possesses few major roads or railways, no national airline, hospitals limited in number and equipment, no emergency housing and little machinery.

If the country concerned was left to cope by itself, there would be even greater loss of life from secondary causes—food shortages, epidemics due to lack of pure water, sanitation and medical supplies, and no shelter. Where floods or drought are involved, it is not simply homes that are lost, but crops and livestock—the means of livelihood. Because there is no government compensation paid and no means of restocking, mass starvation results.

Because of the inability of Third World countries to cope with natural disasters, emergency services have been organized on an international scale.

When disaster strikes

It is possible to organize help for Third World countries in time of natural disaster in a number of ways:

● **Government help** In time of need, it is possible for another country to offer help through its armed services. The RAF often offers transport facilities; the army offers trucks, communications equipment and the services of the medical corps to set up a field hospital. It is sometimes difficult, however, for a country struck by a natural disaster to accept such help, because it is sensitive about having the armed forces of another state on its soil. There is fear of political influence and interference, so that if possible help is found from other sources.

There are political reasons within a country which sometimes cause it to refuse external governmental help. It is claimed, for example, that the Soviet Union will not accept help in time of famine because to do so would show that their centralized planning had failed; or that the Arab nations would not accept help offered for Palestinian refugees, so that their discontent might prove a continuing source of opposition to Israel. Whether or not these particular claims are true, political motives do prevent help from being received from other nations.

● **International organizations**
Many charities, such as the Red

Cross, Oxfam and Christian Aid, are organized on an international basis, and have supplies which can be drawn on in an emergency, as well as personnel who can be used where they are needed. Following a natural disaster in any part of the world, it is also possible for such relief agencies to make financial appeals which bring a quick response from a sympathetic public.

● **The United Nations** The sensitive problem of political influence can be overcome if help and finance is provided through the (neutral) United Nations organizations. Wealthy member countries contribute towards funds so that relief can be given when needed, without any political strings. The Food and Agriculture Organization might help to provide food during an emergency; the World Health Organization would supply medicines and a team of doctors and nurses; UNICEF might help to feed the children and UNESCO would look after their education. When the immediate problems were over, the World Bank might make interest-free loans available to help the Third World country get back on its feet again.

Natural disasters and a God of love?

We have already mentioned that natural disasters are sometimes called 'acts of God' rather than 'acts of nature'. If God is all-loving and all-powerful (as Christians believe), why does he let such disasters happen?

The Bible contains instances of natural disasters being used by God as a means of judgement and punishment (for example, the plagues in Egypt), but also of God preserving his people at times of drought or famine. The Bible shows God clearly in charge of natural forces.

Christians would not pretend to have a clear-cut answer to the problem of reconciling natural disasters and the suffering they cause innocent people with a God of love. However, the following points can be made:
● When God created the world, it was perfect, and that was how he intended it to be. However, when evil came on the scene because of

man's self-will and disobedience, the natural world was affected too. Its original harmony and balance were upset. Natural disasters are a reminder that we live in an imperfect, 'fallen' world.
● We cannot escape the 'geographical realities' of life—certain areas of the world are known to be prone to earthquakes, volcanic activity and the like, because they are on unstable parts of the earth's crust. Living in the 'high risk' areas means that natural disasters are far more likely to strike.
● God does not look on unmoved when a natural disaster causes death and devastation. He is still involved in the world he made, and he suffers when his creatures suffer. He knows what pain, hardship and separation are like, because he came to earth in the person of Jesus, who suffered the agonizing death of crucifixion. So he can share in the feelings of disaster victims.
● Natural disasters are a sobering reminder of the brevity and uncertainty of life, the fact that death can strike anybody at any time. Their occurrence may make us face up to spiritual and eternal realities and encourage us to sort out our own relationship with God.
● Christians would admit that there are some things which just *cannot* be explained. If we could understand everything about God and his thoughts, purposes and activity in the world, we would have reduced him to the level of an ordinary human being. He would hardly be God in that case. Christians would say that they have to accept some things on trust, believing that God knows best. We *do* know that God has an ultimate purpose for the world and mankind, and that he is loving and infinitely concerned for us.
● Even 'out of evil, good may come'. Disasters and the suffering they cause can prompt self-sacrifice and practical caring on the part of those who are moved to help. God's love and compassion can be shown in practical ways in times of natural disaster.

CONSERVATION

Planet earth is like a twentieth-century Noah's Ark, or like a space capsule with plant and animal life and limited supplies of air, water and fuel. Its human family has to take care to see that the occupants survive because resources are limited, and because pollution could kill. A careful balance has to be kept between various forms of plant and animal life or else man's food supplies will be threatened. Even on so large a 'space vehicle' as the earth, care is still needed to see that the human population does not outstrip the available space and resources.

In Units 18 and 21, we have considered the threats to the future of the human race posed by warfare and overpopulation. Many people are also currently concerned about the threat to the planet due to exhaustion of resources, pollution and the extermination of wildlife. Because of the rapidly increasing world population and modern developments in technology, resources are being used up so quickly and waste is being created on so large a scale, that the effects pose a serious threat to human life.

Who cares?

Many people are concerned about these issues. 'Environmentalists' have become an important pressure-group, in politics for instance. But the issues affect everyone: they affect the quality of life not only today but tomorrow as well.

Christians care particularly because they see, too often, the world God has made being spoiled and exploited because of greed or selfishness. They care because the Bible teaches that humankind has been given responsibility for caring for God's creation, developing it and looking after it.

This is a different attitude from

those who just want to conserve the natural world in a wild, undeveloped state. For some, the environment has become a religion: they go out into the countryside and get 'religious' feelings from nature. This is a very romantic view of nature, and makes a 'folk religion' of the created world: Christians believe that we should seek our fulfilment and re-creation in fellowship with God, not oneness with what he has made.

So should we 'conserve' or 'develop'? Do we leave the world in a 'natural' state? In developing it, are we exploiting its resources, polluting and spoiling it?

Resources

The world is running out of some valuable non-renewable resources. This exhaustion is perhaps clearest in the supplies of some of our fuels and minerals.

The manufacture of a car, for example, uses a large number of materials: iron, chromium, lead, silica, copper and zinc. When a car finds its way on to the scrap-heap, the natural materials are lost and cannot be replaced, other than by mining fresh supplies from the earth. There is only a limited amount of each mineral in the earth, so as the usage and wastage continues, the supply is exhausted.

A similar picture is thought to apply to fuel or energy resources. World oil and gas supplies are likely to run out at the end of the twentieth century. A 1980 estimate of coal stocks put remaining supplies at sufficient for over 100 years—hence the attempt to encourage coal consumption in the UK rather than fuels which will soon be exhausted.

Other endangered resources are not quite so obvious. They are renewable, but their natural renewal processes are being affected by man's use of the earth.

Oxygen in the air is vital to life. The amount of oxygen remains constant because of photosynthesis in plants and the action of the sun's rays in decomposing water vapour in the upper atmosphere. However, a current problem is that increasing numbers of people, industrial processes, cars and aircraft are using up more oxygen, while at the same time, deforestation, urbanization and pollution are destroying the very plants which replace the vital oxygen.

Pure water is becoming a scarce resource too. Not only are there more people to use it, but the demands of industry are so great that there is a serious threat of absolute shortage. One estimate of water resources in the USA showed that

they would prove to be inadequate by 1985. This has resulted in a massive water conservation programme being put into effect. Techniques to convert salt water into usable fresh water (desalination) are also being applied in areas of serious shortage, but the energy costs involved are very high.

Even good quality soil—so crucial to food production—can be under threat. As natural windbreaks, such as hedges, are removed to increase the size of fields and facilitate the use of large machines, the speed of the wind across the land increases and valuable topsoil is removed. Farmers have had to strike a balance between efficiency and soil erosion.

Pollution

Pollution takes a number of forms and can spoil the environment in various ways: for example, industrial rubbish or decaying inner cities. Holiday-makers at coastal resorts often find oil from oil-tankers on the beach, rubbish left by other holiday-makers or washed up by the tide, and sewage in the water making it unsafe for swimming. The countryside is often littered with old bedsteads and prams, rusting cans and broken bottles. When you leave a plastic bag behind after a picnic, just think that it could easily suffocate a cow or sheep . . .

Poisoning of the environment is another form of pollution. Land, water and air can all be affected so that they become dangerous to humans and animals. In some areas, where industrial processes leave waste products such as lead and antimony, the soil is poisoned long after the site has been abandoned; the wind may blow the poisoned dust into nearby homes. When crops are sprayed to increase yields by eliminating insect pests, other forms of life are also adversely affected.

Water can become unusable in a number of ways. The discharge of chemicals such as mercury or zinc into rivers kills fish directly, but other, more subtle changes can occur in water. When untreated or excessive amounts of sewage enter a river, the micro-organisms which break down the sewage multiply at an incredible rate. They need so

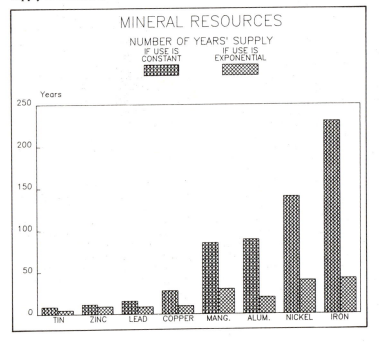

MINERAL RESOURCES

NUMBER OF YEARS' SUPPLY

IF USE IS CONSTANT   IF USE IS EXPONENTIAL

Years

250

200

150

100

50

0

TIN   ZINC   LEAD   COPPER   MANG.   ALUM.   NICKEL   IRON

much oxygen that the oxygen content of the water is lowered and other creatures die.

No air is really 'pure': air consists of a mixture of gases, water vapour and dust. It is when the air does harm that it is called impure or polluted.

Most pollution takes place because of a high concentration of poisonous gases in the air. The gases are released as a result of combustion. In the UK, smokeless zones have removed the hazards of smog.

The real pollution culprit is industry. The concentration of dust

Methods of agriculture practised in some parts of the Third World turn the country into a desert. 'Slash and burn' clearing of land for crop-growing impoverishes the soil. When yields become too low to make farming worthwhile, the site is abandoned and the process repeated elsewhere. The land loses its natural protection of trees or bushes, soil erosion takes place and 'dust bowl' conditions may be created.

from industrial processes such as cement manufacture can be so high that growing things are smothered, and the effect of sunlight is reduced. Sulphur dioxide is given off in many industrial processes, and this combines with moisture in the atmosphere to form dilute sulphuric acid. The acid not only attacks the outside of buildings, but it also causes lung damage to people and stunts plant growth.

The fluorocarbons in aerosol cans are said to rise into the atmosphere and destroy the ozone layer, which protects the earth from harmful ultra-violet radiation.

Wildlife

In one sense, the whole planet is a large, integrated ecosystem. If any part of it is tampered with, damaged or destroyed, there are repercussions throughout the whole system because of the way that all forms of life are connected.

Some experts have suggested that the earth faces disaster because the global ecosystem is being tampered with. They are referring to such things as the production of more waste than can be coped with or recycled; to pollution and exhaustion of resources which are needed by living creatures. But they are also concerned about the elimination of some forms of wildlife, which had important links with other creatures in the system.

Animals are under threat for a

YOU HAVE BEEN WARNED!

● **Rubbish** We live in a 'throw-away' society—manufacturers make throw-away containers because it is too expensive for them to reuse the materials. They make goods which wear out quickly so that sales are maintained. In the UK each year, we dispose of 10,000 million paper bags, 6,000 million glass containers, 375 million aerosols and 20 million tyres. Our rubbish costs over £200 million per year to be collected and disposed of. The rubbish has to be transported greater distances at greater cost, or it is taken out to sea and dumped there.
● **Fumes** A serious form of air pollution is the gas produced by car exhausts. As well as carbon monoxide, the fumes contain lead; if this reaches dangerous levels, it may slow down brain development in young children. High traffic density and unique climatic conditions have made Los Angeles notorious for its poisonous smog,

which cannot escape into the atmosphere. In Tokyo, police on traffic duty have to wear protective masks to counteract the harmful effects of exhaust fumes.
● **Noise** The world we live in is becoming increasingly noisy through the use of machinery, vehicles and amplifiers. Noise pollution can also be harmful. Sound volume is measured in decibels (db), on a scale representing the smallest change in volume of sound which can be detected by the human ear. Silence therefore = 0db; whispering = 20db, talking = 40db, a vacuum cleaner 60db, and a loud radio or heavy traffic 80db. A circular saw registers 100 + db and Concorde 120db. Noise above 180db causes death; noise at 130db can cause permanent deafness. People working in factories, operating machinery, attending discos or living by major roads can actually be physically harmed by noise pollution.
● **Plants and animals** Certain wild flower species—among others the

soldier orchid, alpine gentian, Snowdon lily and Killarney fern—are under threat of extinction. They need to be protected and preserved, as they can never be replaced once lost.

Some forms of animal life became extinct because they failed to adapt successfully to their environment—for example, *tyrannosaurus rex,* the dodo, moa, great auk and quagga. Their disappearance does not seem to have caused a major disaster. However, the problem today is different in scale: the sheer number of species which are disappearing, and the speed at which this is happening, has given rise to alarm. The balance of the ecosystem is under threat. In the first half of the twentieth century, about fifty species of mammal disappeared. Endangered species which are the object of current international concern include the mountain gorilla, Asiatic lion, tiger, Javan rhino, blue whale, green turtle and panda.

number of reasons:

● **Destruction of habitat** A 'habitat' is the natural home of a plant or animal. Habitat can be destroyed in many ways: building roads and cities, removing hedges, draining marshland, overgrazing uncultivated land, cultivating former wilderness areas, pollution of beaches, wars.

Habitat can also be destroyed less obviously: when new creatures are introduced into an area and there are no natural predators, they may eat the vegetation needed by other creatures; or the newcomers may become so numerous that similar creatures are driven out. This happened when the rabbit was introduced into Australia and when the grey squirrel was introduced into the UK.

When chemicals such as DDT are used to eliminate harmful pests, the food supply for other creatures might be destroyed or contaminated at the same time—once again, the habitat or natural home has disappeared.

● **Desire for animal skins** The coats and feathers of many living creatures are very beautiful, and there has always been a demand for fur, feathers and skins to make clothes. Animals have been slaughtered by high-powered weapons to such an extent *solely for fashion* that many species of animal have almost disappeared. Chinchillas, fur seals, foxes, tigers and leopards have all been under threat.

● **Desire for animal meat** Animals have been slaughtered to meet the food needs of a rapidly expanding population. The days when herds of buffalo roamed the North American plains are long gone. In 1953, there were about 10,000 blue whales in existence—today there are very few left. They have been hunted by fleets of modern factory ships, and have been killed because their vast bodies were valuable for soap, cosmetics and pet food, as well as meat (a popular delicacy in Japan). There is at present serious concern about overfishing in the North Sea. So many fish are being caught, that the remaining stock may not be able to reproduce effectively.

● **Sport** Many animals have been killed because it was believed that they were dangerous to man. The element of danger led to the idea that killing a wild animal was good sport. Hunting for food also became hunting for sport.

In days when bows and arrows were used, and when there was an element of danger for the hunter, the killing of wildlife was not so serious. But now that high-powered weapons

CONNECTIONS

All forms of life on earth are connected in an intricate web of relationships, like a chain with interlocking links. To upset one link is to risk destroying the whole chain. Because of this interdependence, it is vital to understand and maintain the delicate balance between all living creatures—humans included.

The food chain

All energy comes to us ultimately from the sun, but plants alone can use this energy to convert it to food by photosynthesis. Lower forms of animal life have to eat plants to obtain food—they are called **primary consumers**. Higher forms of animal life feed on creatures lower down the hierarchy (although they may eat plants as well); they are called **secondary consumers**. The sun's energy is therefore transferred from plants to other creatures by eating. The steps in this process are called a **food chain**.

Leaves→earthworms→blackbirds→ sparrowhawks
Grain→chicken (eggs)→humans
Algae→water fleas→minnows→pike→ herons→foxes
Grass→cows (milk)→humans

There are a number of important factors to bear in mind about food chains:

● **Energy loss** When a cow eats grass, most of the energy it obtains is lost in breathing, body processes and waste. Only a small amount is actually used for growth. It is therefore much more economical for man to eat plants (i.e. vegetables, grains and pulses) than for him to eat meat. This is of great importance in sharing out the world's food resources (see Unit 19, Poverty).

● **Pyramid of numbers** The higher one goes up the food chain, the fewer creatures there are. For example, there are billions of algae, millions of water fleas, thousands of minnows, hundreds of pike . . . In a balanced system, a creature has to feed on many creatures below it in the chain in order to obtain the energy it needs. This 'pyramid' has important implications for the accumulation of poisons. When creatures low down the chain are poisoned by pollution at a level which they can survive, their body-poison becomes more concentrated in their predators—perhaps to an extent which the (fewer) creatures at the higher level cannot survive.

● **Broken food chains** If creatures are eliminated *at any point* in the chain, the whole balance of life is at risk. If, for example, foxes and herons were hunted out of existence, the pike population might explode to the point where minnows disappeared. Not only would this lead to the loss of minnows, but the pike population would ultimately be reduced by starvation, rather than by the elimination of the weakest. The whole stock would be affected.

The ecosystem

Life relationships are much more complex than the food chains. Sparrowhawks eat food other than blackbirds; man eats more than eggs. And what is more, plant life is dependent upon animal life, and not just vice versa. When animals breathe, they exhale carbon dioxide which is needed by plants. When animals get rid of waste, it is broken down by bacteria into a form needed by plant life.

Each area in which plant life, water, animals, air and soil are interconnected and in balance is called an **ecosystem**. When man therefore interferes with an ecosystem by influencing any part of it, he can upset the whole web of relationships in a very dramatic way. Because he is part of the system, he may put his own life in danger too. God's original purpose was that man should 'manage' the natural world— develop and use it responsibly, taking care of all aspects of his environment. Only in this way can the whole system function as intended (see also 'What the Bible says').

are available, the wild animal has little chance.

● **Demand for live animals**
Thousands of animals are trapped each year so that they can be used for laboratory experiments. Apes and monkeys are particularly valuable for research because they share many characteristics with man. Some of the research done is for valid medical reasons, but some uses animals for purposes of questionable value—for example, to develop and test new cosmetics.

Programme for survival

Environmental and conservation issues have only become major headline news since about 1970. In 1972, a group calling itself The Club of Rome drew attention to the seriousness of the situation worldwide, and published a book, *The Limits to Growth*, detailing the problems of population growth, resource depletion, environmental pollution and the limits to food yields. The American authors recommended certain courses of action. This acted as a trigger to many people who were concerned about similar issues, and conservation and ecology groups sprang up to highlight the dangers and to try to prevent further damage. In some cases, this has been done with the help of local and national government, and even on an international scale.

Considerable progress has been made in certain areas, although much remains to be done. Achievements over recent years have included:
● national parks, nature reserves and safari parks established as protected areas;
● fish have returned to the River Thames in London after the introduction of measures controlling the discharge of poisonous effluents;
● smokeless zones declared, putting an end to dangerous smogs;
● fluorocarbons banned for non-essential uses in USA;
● international agreement to ban commercial whaling from 1985;
● 1972: first ever international conference on the Human Environment held in Stockholm,

'RESCUE SERVICES'

● **The Conservation Society** (228 London Road, Reading, Berkshire RG6 1AH) is a charity set up in 1970 to promote understanding of factors which affect population, natural resources and the human environment, by means of publications, news-letters and lectures.
● **Friends of the Earth** (377 City Road, London EC1V 1MA) is another movement set up to educate people about conservation problems and the waste of resources. It is a pressure group which organizes campaigns against commercial interests which appear to be careless of the world and its resources: for example, it has opposed copper-mining in Snowdonia, the use of non-returnable bottles, the slaughter of whales, the use of nuclear fuels, increasing the size of lorries allowed on roads, etc.
● **The National Trust** (42 Queen Anne's Gate, London SW1H 9AS) was established as a charity in 1895 to help to preserve Britain's national heritage: houses, commercial buildings, gardens, coastline and countryside of historic, artistic and natural importance

are purchased and administered by the Trust. Young people can volunteer for training in conservation work at Acorn Camps, and local groups raise funds and work at NT properties.
● **The Nature Conservancy Council** (19 Belgrave Square, London SW1X 9PG) is a government body which seeks to promote nature conservation nationwide. It is responsible for establishing nature reserves and publishes reports on conservation based on research and surveys.
● **The World Wildlife Fund** (Wildlife, Wallington, Surrey SM6 0DN) is an international charity whose objective is to stimulate appreciation of nature and wildlife so as to encourage their protection. Its UK youth wing is the Panda Club UK.
● **The Royal Society for the Protection of Birds** (The Lodge, Sandy, Bedfordshire SG19 2DL) is concerned specifically with protecting bird life from environmental threats: destruction of habitats, danger from oil slicks, etc. It sponsors research, manages eighty-seven reserves in Britain, and conducts counts to determine numbers of certain endangered species.

attended by delegates from 120 countries;
● reforestation programmes;
● banning of use of certain pesticides and defoliants;
● research into solar/tidal/wind energy and energy-saving schemes.

Some people are calling for some kind of international control, such as a 'world environment authority'. Others believe that self-control is the

best solution, and are seeking to bring it about by shocking people into a knowledge of the situation: if people understand the dangers (so it is said), they will be willing to adopt a simpler life-style. If people in rich countries consume less, this will have the added advantage of improving their health!

Although public awareness of the environmental crisis has been

ACTION PLAN

● Consider eating less meat—better for your health plus the fact that meat (especially beef) requires a lot of grain to produce.
● Try eating less food altogether! Most of us eat more than we actually need.
● Save paper used on only one side for future use for notes, etc.
● Save envelopes for re-use, resealing them with labels sold by many of the conservation organizations.
● Take old newspapers and magazines to local collecting depot or group (if there is one) for recycling.
● Have showers instead of baths—the

less water you use, the more fuel is saved at the pumping station.
● Don't leave lights or heaters on in unused rooms.
● Buy drinks and other liquids in returnable bottles if possible. Take non-returnable bottles to a 'bottle bank' for recycling.
● Try to avoid the use of aerosol sprays—they pollute both the air and our lungs, and are very difficult to dispose of.
● Don't just throw things away—look after your possessions, make them last and think who else could benefit if you have finished with something (books, clothes, records . . .).

WHAT THE BIBLE SAYS

'So God created human beings, making them to be like himself. He created them male and female, blessed them, and said, "Have many children, so that your descendants will live all over the earth and bring it under their control. I am putting you in charge of the fish, the birds, and all the wild animals. I have provided all kinds of grain and all kinds of fruit for you to eat; but for all the wild animals and for all the birds I have provided grass and leafy plants for food"—and it was done.' (Genesis 1:27–30)

'You appointed him [man] ruler over everything you made; you placed him over all creation: sheep and cattle, and the wild animals too; the birds and the fish and the creatures in the sea.' (Psalm 8:6–8)

God put mankind in charge of creation. He is to manage its resources. Man is ultimately responsible to God—he has the role of a 'steward' or manager, who should use wisely what has been entrusted to him. He should work with nature, not against it, and try to understand it, not ignore, despise or exploit it.

★ ★ ★

'"For six years sow your field and gather in what it produces. But in the seventh year let it rest, and do not harvest anything that grows on it. The poor may eat what grows there, and the wild animals can have what is left. Do the same with your vineyards and your olive-trees."' (Exodus 23:10–11)

God's laws to the Israelites contained specific instructions about the use of resources—soil exhaustion was avoided by a 'fallow year', and the poor in the community and the wild animals benefited from the natural growth in that year.

★ ★ ★

'"When you are trying to capture a city, do not cut down its fruit-trees, even though the siege lasts a long time. Eat the fruit, but do not destroy the trees; the trees are not your enemies . . . If you happen to find a bird's nest in a tree or on the ground with the mother bird sitting either on the eggs or with her young, you are not to take the mother bird."' (Deuteronomy 20:19; 22:6)

God's people were taught to have respect for nature.

★ ★ ★

'Since you have plenty at this time, it is only fair that you should help those who are in need. Then, when you are in need and they have plenty, they will help you . . . As the scripture says, "The one who gathered much did not have too much, and the one who gathered little did not have too little."' (2 Corinthians 8:14–15)

Christians should share resources with those in need.

★ ★ ★

'Love your neighbour as you love yourself.' (Luke 10:27)

The neighbour-love that Jesus taught and lived out is the guiding principle for Christians, and an example to everyone. The power that Jesus gives can transform selfish attitudes. Christians may feel that they should make changes in their life-style if their way of life is adversely affecting other people—whether the 'neighbour' is in a poorer country across the world or a 'neighbour' still to be born, who may come into a world threatened by environmental disaster.

increased and some progress has been made, some people wonder whether man can *ever* solve the problem of an overpopulated, polluted and exhausted planet. This is because they feel that the real cause of the problem lies much deeper than the solutions so far suggested deal with.

What makes people exploit non-renewable resources when they know that it will affect succeeding generations? What makes people want animal skins for clothes when they know that this endangers certain species? What makes a local authority discharge sewage into the estuary, or a factory manager discharge poison into the river, or a ship's captain discharge oil into the sea when each of them knows the harm they are doing? Why does a farmer uproot hedges, knowing that this destroys natural habitats? Why does a manufacturer produce goods which do not last or are produced in non-returnable containers?

The answer would seem to be that human greed, selfishness and laziness lie behind many of the world's problems of waste, pollution and exploitation. The desire to make a profit, to avoid personal inconvenience and expense, or to gratify a selfish whim overrule any considerations about how a particular action will affect people or nature, either in the short or long term. As someone has said, the most dangerous 'animal' on the planet is man!

Christians support scientific research, technological development and the harnessing of natural resources for mankind's benefit. They believe in developing the world and its resources, not just allowing it to 'lie fallow' or run wild. At the same time they urge restraint and conservation (on a personal, national and international level) in the use of God's world. They believe that the new life Jesus Christ offers can change people's deep-seated attitudes

of selfishness, and that this change of heart holds the key to responsible use of the environment.

Discussion topics

1 Do you think it matters what kind of world we leave behind for future generations?

2 'In a world where hundreds of millions confront absolute poverty, those of us who enjoy relative abundance must learn to live more simply.' Do you agree?

3 How could you make your own life-style less wasteful?

4 What efforts are made in your local community to tackle problems of waste and pollution? Are you involved in any of them?

5 Do you agree with the Christian assessment of the environmental crisis—that it is a symptom of human greed and selfishness?